THE ENCYCLOPEDIA OF
CARTOONING
TECHNIQUES

THE ENCYCLOPEDIA OF
CARTOONING
TECHNIQUES

STEVE WHITAKER
CONSULTANT EDITOR STEVE EDGELL

RUNNING PRESS
PHILADELPHIA · LONDON

ISBN 1-56138-354-6

Library of Congress Cataloging-in-
Publication Number: 93-87585

This book was designed and produced by
Quarto Publishing Inc
The Old Brewery
6 Blundell Street
London N7 9BH

Senior editor Kate Kirby
Editors Judy Martin, Hazel Harrison
Art editors Clare Baggaley, Mark Stevens
Designers Patrick Knowles, Penny Dawes
Picture researchers Sarah Risley, Laura Bangert
Photographer Chas Wilder
Picture manager Giulia Hetherington
Editorial director Sophie Collins
Art director Moira Clinch

Typeset by Central Southern Typesetters, Eastbourne
Manufactured in Singapore by Eray Scan Pte Ltd
Printed in Singapore by Star Standard
Industries (Pte) Ltd

This book may be ordered by mail from the publisher.
Please include $2.50 for postage and handling. *But try your
bookstore first!*

Running Press Book Publishers
125 South Twenty-second Street
Philadelphia, Pennsylvania 19103-4399

CONTENTS

TECHNIQUES
PAGE 22

THEMES
PAGE 124

FOREWORD

It's an odd life being a cartoonist. On first hearing that you earn your living drawing pictures, people usually react with a mixture of disbelief and reverence. So, after you've established that there's no "proper" job you do besides cartooning, you'll often get a sort of confession that goes something like, "Of course, I can't draw." Take my word for it, everyone can draw.

The same set of ideas that makes it so out of keeping for an everyday person to do something as mysterious and magical as drawing for a living also makes it seem unachievable. But the simple fact is that we have our sights set too high. We're taught that, as "art," drawing is a highly specialized skill that no one but an expert can – or should – practice. But if you can put an idea or an observation across in a drawing – no matter how simple it is – then you are a cartoonist. Expecting every cartoon to be smooth and accomplished is as nonsensical as saying that all handwriting has to be neat.

So a cartoon is, simply put, a drawing that says something. This is not the way the word was always understood. Originally a cartoon was a full-sized preparatory drawing for a wall painting, a tapestry, or occasionally a mosaic. The word comes from "cartone," the pasteboard the Italians used for such drawings in the 14th and 15th centuries. It wasn't until about 250 years ago that satirical drawings and humorous caricatures began to be called cartoons. Advances in popular printing made sure of their continued acceptance in newspapers and pamphlets. By the end of the 19th century the illustrated narrative had evolved into the comic strip – a story where the words became part of each picture. Despite all the upheaval of this century, the simple cartoon is still with us. In newspapers, magazines, and advertisements, and on T-shirts, the need to make a picture that has something to say continues.

The purpose of this book is to provide as comprehensive a selection of ways and means to cartoon as possible. The encyclopedia is divided into three sections. The first section gives a comprehensive analysis of drawing materials available to the cartoonist. The second section, Techniques, provides in-depth coverage of cartooning techniques and basic principles. This section is divided alphabetically by technique and cross-refers, where appropriate, to other related techniques. Included here is an entry on presentation and publication – for those of you who want to make a stab at earning some money. Section three, Themes, comprises a gallery of professional drawings arranged in five genres: satire and comment, caricature, humor, strips, and cartoon illustration, with a critical commentary on each drawing. Whether your interest lies in being professional or amateur, be prepared for that semi-amazed look you'll get from people when you tell them what you do. It really is a funny old life being a cartoonist. Have fun!

Steve Whitaker

Steve Whitaker

GETTING STARTED

THIS SECTION LOOKS AT BASIC TOOLS AND MATERIALS USED BY THE PROFESSIONAL CARTOONIST, ENABLING A CONFIDENT AND APPROPRIATE CHOICE OF MEDIUM AND SUBSTRATE.

TOOLS
&
EQUIPMENT

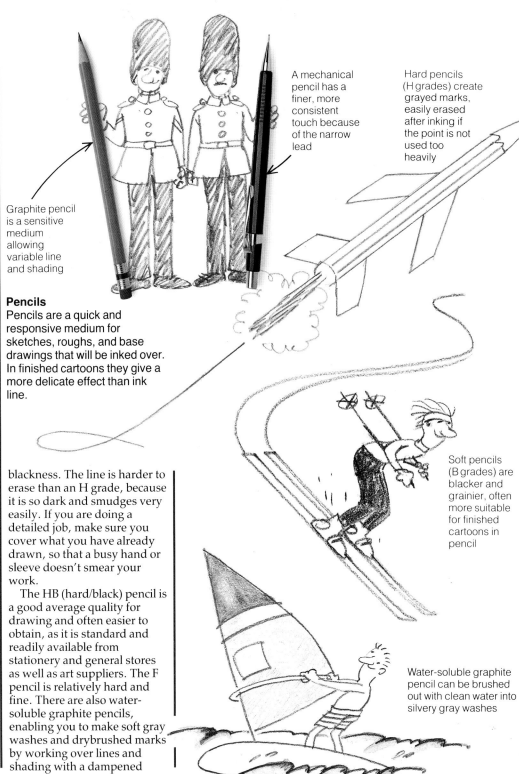

Graphite pencil is a sensitive medium allowing variable line and shading

A mechanical pencil has a finer, more consistent touch because of the narrow lead

Hard pencils (H grades) create grayed marks, easily erased after inking if the point is not used too heavily

Soft pencils (B grades) are blacker and grainier, often more suitable for finished cartoons in pencil

Water-soluble graphite pencil can be brushed out with clean water into silvery gray washes

Cartoons can be produced in all kinds of media, techniques, and styles, but they are largely associated with black-and-white drawings, so consider using these media first.

Pencils
You have a choice between traditional wood-cased pencils or mechanical pencils. Pencil leads are basically hard (H) or soft (B for black). The "lead" is graphite, or a mixture of graphite and clay.

Some artists prefer the H pencil because it makes a very slight, gray line, but being hard, the lead tends to score the paper if used too heavily or energetically. This can be a problem when ink is to be applied to a drawing, since a damaged paper surface can lead to blots and ink bleeding from the lines (especially on board). If you are confident and have a clean, immediate style, an H pencil should suit you. Pencils are graded numerically; the higher the number (2H, 3H, 4H) the harder and grayer the lead.

Other artists prefer B pencils (graded from 2B to 8B) because they create very black lines useful for emphasis. If you want to produce a finished cartoon in pencil, the B lead is recommended for its

Pencils
Pencils are a quick and responsive medium for sketches, roughs, and base drawings that will be inked over. In finished cartoons they give a more delicate effect than ink line.

blackness. The line is harder to erase than an H grade, because it is so dark and smudges very easily. If you are doing a detailed job, make sure you cover what you have already drawn, so that a busy hand or sleeve doesn't smear your work.

The HB (hard/black) pencil is a good average quality for drawing and often easier to obtain, as it is standard and readily available from stationery and general stores as well as art suppliers. The F pencil is relatively hard and fine. There are also water-soluble graphite pencils, enabling you to make soft gray washes and drybrushed marks by working over lines and shading with a dampened brush. If your cartoon is going into print, a pencil drawing is best reproduced as a halftone image, to pick up the subtleties in the surface textures.

Mechanical pencils are refillable and designed to take a variety of leads, in thicknesses from 0.3–0.9mm increasing in 0.2mm increments. The advantage of a mechanical pencil is that it is "sharp" all the time, so the lead widths give you the choice of how delicate or sensitive you want the pencil point to be. Soft leads break easily, but the hard grades are very brittle. Most artists use 0.5 or 0.7, but a soft 0.9 is useful for roughs, layouts, or sketching. The clutch pencil takes relatively thick leads that are also well-suited to broader drawing.

Dip pens

The traditional implement of the cartoonist is still the dip pen. Unfortunately, there is no simple method for starting to draw perfectly with a dip pen right away. The critical factor is comfort – you need to be comfortable with a pen in order to use it confidently. There are various pen nibs to be recommended for various line qualities. The nib should be flexible, durable, adaptable, and reliably consistent.

To begin with, obtain a writing pen rather than a drawing or mapping pen, with a pointed nib such as those used for copperplate writing (not a squared italic nib). When you have found out what you like about using a dip pen, then you can begin to specialize and try some of the standard pen nibs used by cartoonists.

There are essentially two

A fountain pen handles easily and the non-waterproof ink gives some tonal variation in the line

A pointed dip pen nib, ideal for beginners

A technical pen, handled upright, is designed to provide a fine, very consistent mark

Dip pens are versatile; varying the pressure and direction of the nib alters line weight and texture

A pointed drawing pen nib needs to be firm but flexible

sorts of penholder – short or long. Much the same as with brush handles, some artists like a long handle with a little weight at the top to balance the working end (some even weight the handle by attaching a ball of masking tape); others prefer a short handle, which has the advantage of being easier to fit into a pencil case or pocket. There are attachments for larger or smaller nibs, so if you intend to use a variety of pen points, make sure you have a holder that is adaptable to your choice of nib.

Fountain pens

These are comfortable to use and commercial ranges include a number of good pens for drawing. The main drawback of fountain pens is that the ink used in them is not waterproof. Waterproof inks

rapidly clog the pen and should not be used. There are one or two permanent, free-flow inks designed for use in fountain pens, less dense than India ink but more versatile in this context.

The range of nibs is limited. There is no fountain pen nib that can match the fineness of a mapping pen or the flexibility of most dip pens. You will need to work broadly and on a suitable scale – nothing too tiny or delicately detailed.

Technical pens

These pens have been developed to give a perfect line for ruling borders and straight edges in graphic work. The "nib" is a tiny metal pipe that channels the ink; sizes range from as small as 0.1mm up to a bold 2mm. Because of the mechanical consistency of the point, technical pens do not lend themselves to expressive drawing. However, the same characteristic makes them the perfect tools for even stippling.

11

Brushes

You need to keep two types of brush, a brush for drawing and one or more for applying color. Many people find it very uncomfortable to draw with a brush, because you have less control over the splaying hairs than over a compact pen nib. As with any drawing implement, comfort is the most important element, and this will determine whether you prefer a big, bulbous brush with a fine point that can take up lots of ink or a tiny "dagger-point" sable 00 brush. You should also consider whether you like a short handle or a long one that weighs against your drawing movement.

Roundhair sable brushes, available in sizes 000 to 12, are relatively expensive, but for drawing are the most responsive. Synthetic brushes and acrylic/sable mixes are springier and can flick the ink where you don't want it. When using waterproof black ink, remember to clean the brush very thoroughly down to the metal ferrule, otherwise the ink rots the hairs. Use ordinary soap if you cannot clean it thoroughly with water – dishwashing detergent is unsuitable because it is gritty.

For filling large areas of black, a larger synthetic-hair brush is handy and time-saving. Some professionals use cotton swabs for this kind of work, which give a splendid finish.

Keep your old, worn-down drawing brushes. They come in useful for drybrush techniques that involve spreading and dragging the brush hairs, which may spoil a sable brush for finer drawing.

Brushes for applying opaque color and washes need not be sable, but should have a similar feel (bristle brushes are only suitable for work in acrylic or oil). Keep a fine brush for detailing and a broader one for filling in large areas. Roundhair brushes are usually preferred, but you may find a squared brush useful for filling hard-edged shapes. Add to these a "mop" – a big soft watercolorists' brush used for wetting the paper to receive color washes. This is good for laying down a sweep of flat or blended color, such as a background or sky.

As with drawing brushes, select the type and size that suits your own needs. Keep in mind that the longer the brush hairs, the more color they retain, which can be crucial in applying color washes accurately.

An old brush that has splayed is still useful

A cotton swab is an excellent tool for laying solid colors

Brushes for drawing must be good quality types that are flexible and maintain a clean point

For washes of tone and color, choose a large roundhair brush from watercolor ranges

Use a waterproof, densely black ink for work in line and wash.

Drawing and writing inks are adequate for line only

Non-waterproof ink   Writing ink   Drawing pen ink

Brushes

Good drawing and wash brushes are relatively expensive, but the quality of the tool will be reflected in the tone and texture of your work – a poor brush makes a poor mark.

Drawing inks

The most important aspect of a black drawing ink is whether or not it is waterproof. The dried ink line work must not be soluble if you are going to lay color washes into your drawing. India ink, also called "encre de Chine", is the best, but make sure it is fully waterproof as some specially ground non-waterproof types are sold under the same name.

Markers are available with wedge- or chisel-shaped tips, thick bullet points, or fine fiber-tips

Markers are comfortable for free, simple cartooning styles and a thick tip gives a lively directional line

Markers and mechanical tints
Markers (above) can be used for roughs, ideas sheets, and finished cartoons. Mechanical tints (right) add even tone to ink line drawing.

Black-dot mechanical tints offer a range of fine and coarse patterns that read as varied "gray" tones

Self-adhesive or dry-transfer mechanical tints are trimmed to shape on the artwork

There are other specialist inks of extreme blackness available, under a variety of brand names. Buy a large bottle – it is more economical and means you will not run out of medium in the middle of a drawing. Before you use the ink, take the lid off and let the bottle stand for a day or two. The ink thickens slightly so you do not encounter the usual watery consistency at the top.

Markers
This term can include all kinds of felt- and fiber-tip pens with drawing tips from very fine to very broad. Many black marker inks are water-based and are not truly black, but a mixture of blue and orange. This is important if you are doing work for reproduction; a process camera does not see blue as well as other colors, and this tends to weaken any line work done in water-based ink. Spirit-based inks are blacker and semi-permanent; they reproduce well and you can lay color washes over them.

Markers usually have a limited range of expression where line quality is concerned, but their convenience value is high and they are much quicker and easier than dip pens for drawing roughs and layouts.

Mechanical tints
Many cartoonists like to add gray tone to their drawings when they are limited to black-and-white reproduction. While pen and wash is an acceptable cartooning style, shooting the artwork in halftone can be expensive and/or beyond the capabilities of the print method or format.

Prepared mechanical tints are a practical alternative – basically, black dot patterns that reproduce as even grays. The "grain" and size of the dot patterns vary, so you can have deep, dense grays or a more open, luminous tone. The concentration ranges from 10 percent to 90 percent black, and different measures of dots per square inch. The cruder your proposed printing method, the bolder the dot screen you need. Printing can darken the fine tones, so use 10 or 20 percent for an average gray.

Mechanical tints are self-adhesive sheets (you peel off a backing paper as you lay them down) or dry-transfer dots; you need a burnisher to rub them down evenly. Dry-transfer tones should be cut larger than the area you need and trimmed to the precise outline after application (use a very sharp frisket knife blade and a light touch). Don't use the self-adhesive types on photocopied drawings, as the sticky back of the tint film can lift the photocopied line.

You can also obtain a variety of patterns, and also color tint sheets, which are both valuable and time-saving for decorative or formal styles of work where completely even tones are an asset.

Colors

You can choose from a variety of media and methods for coloring your cartoon. If your work is for print, there may be special requirements on medium, presentation, and finish, so make sure you get a detailed brief. The following are the main color media, with comments on their advantages and disadvantages.

Watercolor

Available as semi-moist cakes (pans) or in tube form, and in a vast color range, high-quality artists' watercolors are expensive but usually worth the extra cost. A box of water-color pans is good back-up for studio or location work, and easily portable. Tube colors are easier to use for broad washes. Unless you are well practiced in watercolor wash technique, avoid very large color areas or ambitious gradations, as they can come out looking very patchy and dabbed when reproduced.

Dyes and inks

Dyes are very fine liquid color with nothing added, so you are literally dyeing the paper you are coloring. This is very friendly to the process camera. Colored inks contain a water-proofing medium so, while they stay where they are on the paper as they dry, the medium usually limits how much mixing around you can do.

Several manufacturers now make liquid acrylic colors that are designed to intermix, with an admirable color range. If you have dyes and acrylic colors, you can do a lot of the work with the dyes before adding glazes of waterproof color.

Liquid colors have been specially formulated for artwork intended for reproduction. Their permanency is not always guaranteed, as is the lightfast-ness of artists' watercolors. Check the manufacturer's rating for permanency if you want your original cartoon to last.

Gouache and poster paint

Poster paint is a very crude water-based paint that tends to crack if applied thickly. It contains a lot of filler, and the colors can look fairly dead. It is not recommended for work to be reproduced, but is fine for roughs.

Gouache is opaque water-color; the inclusion of white pigment makes all the colors opaque. The colors lighten and can change noticeably as they dry, which takes some getting used to. Gouache is formulated to dry flat, and you have to dilute it very thinly to get it to behave otherwise. Artists'-quality gouache tube paints come in an incredible range of colors. Some artists like to use gouache for heavily modeled images, but you may find it easier to work that way with acrylic paints.

Acrylic and oil paints

Oil paint is rarely used for cartoons but if you try it, work on a canvas paper or board specially made for oils. It can be difficult to control, as the medium remains wet and movable for such a long time. Acrylic paint is more convenient and being water-based, eliminates the oily and unpleasant-smelling thinners that you have to use with oils. Acrylics dry to a tough plastic "skin" and are ideal if your cartoon needs some heavily painted modeling and texture, or if the image has to be permanent and durable.

If you do not wish to invest in a full set of acrylics, for occasional use you can obtain similar effects using acrylic medium mixed into gouache.

Pastels, crayons, and colored pencils

These media are sometimes referred to as "dry color," and

Dye colors are fluid and intense

Poster paints have a limited, unsubtle color range compared to watercolors or gouache

A small box of watercolor pans is a convenient color source

Drawing inks provide bright, translucent color, but some brands have a limited color range

Tube watercolors are formulated for easy dilution and flow

that is both their strength and weakness. If you apply dry color to a picture with any kind of texture to it (including erased pencil lines that sometimes score the paper deeper than you'd expect), it exaggerates that texture and usually leaves little uncovered specks of the paper color. The effect is a little like stippling; the flecks slow the eye down and give a static look to the image. If you use pastels or colored pencils, try applying them to tinted paper.

On the positive side, dry color is in itself a great textural device – if you want something to look dry, crumbly or sandy, for example – and pastels can emulate close-up skin texture very well.

Pastels come in three varieties: chalk or soft pastels, which are powdery and have to be fixed; oil pastels, which are like greasy, opaque wax crayons; and water-soluble pastels, opaque or waxy, which combine the durability of oil pastel with the sensitivity of chalk.

Colored pencils range from hard, fine leads to soft velvety or chalky textures, to water-soluble types that can be used dry or wet.

Wax crayons do not reproduce well, since the color is merely suspended in transparent wax which is smeared onto the paper. But they are useful as wax-resist with water-soluble media for irregular effects of color and texture.

Markers
There are huge ranges of color markers in hundreds of shades and tones, as well as different-sized tips. These are made for designers and people in a hurry and, as convenience items, are very expensive. All you really need is a watercolor box or some inks, and markers are not ideal for cartoonists starting out, though they are a quick and easy option for roughs and layouts.

However, there is a look to marker coloring that has become acceptable – check out color cartoons in the more upscale, glossy magazines. And if you start to get commissioned work, you may find certain marker ranges useful in that they can match specified color requirements for print.

Gouache is an opaque paint that can be applied thickly without dilution or as a thin, slightly "chalky" wash

Soft pastels remain powdery on the paper and a pastel drawing needs to be fixed

Oil pastels are a juicy, quick-to-work medium for freely textured color

Acrylics make a tough, glossy surface effect but can be thinned in transparent washes

Slow-drying oil paint is an unusual medium for cartooning

Colored pencil ranges include hard and soft, waxy, dry, and chalky textures as well as water-soluble colors

Marker color can have a speedy look, as the movement of the marker tip often remains visible

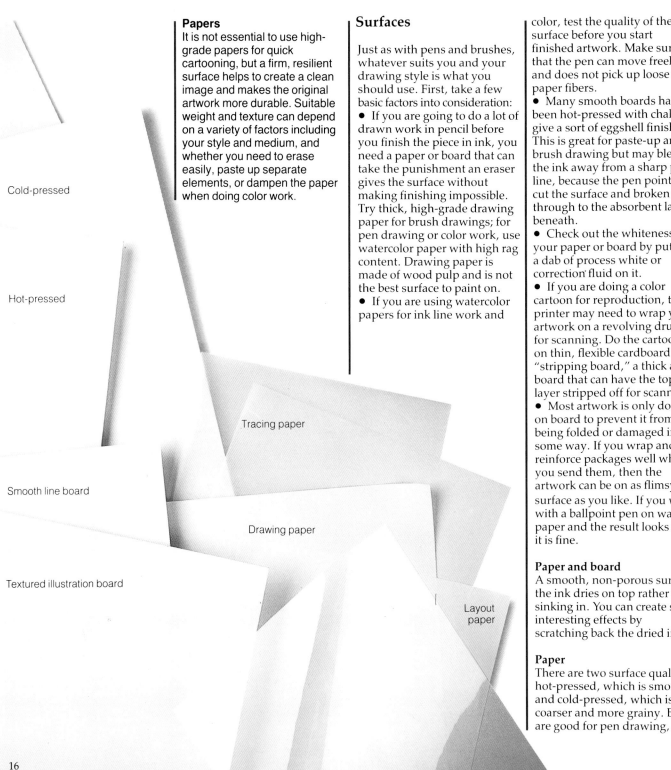

Cold-pressed

Hot-pressed

Tracing paper

Smooth line board

Drawing paper

Textured illustration board

Layout paper

Papers

It is not essential to use high-grade papers for quick cartooning, but a firm, resilient surface helps to create a clean image and makes the original artwork more durable. Suitable weight and texture can depend on a variety of factors including your style and medium, and whether you need to erase easily, paste up separate elements, or dampen the paper when doing color work.

Surfaces

Just as with pens and brushes, whatever suits you and your drawing style is what you should use. First, take a few basic factors into consideration:

• If you are going to do a lot of drawn work in pencil before you finish the piece in ink, you need a paper or board that can take the punishment an eraser gives the surface without making finishing impossible. Try thick, high-grade drawing paper for brush drawings; for pen drawing or color work, use watercolor paper with high rag content. Drawing paper is made of wood pulp and is not the best surface to paint on.

• If you are using watercolor papers for ink line work and color, test the quality of the surface before you start finished artwork. Make sure that the pen can move freely and does not pick up loose paper fibers.

• Many smooth boards have been hot-pressed with chalk to give a sort of eggshell finish. This is great for paste-up and brush drawing but may bleed the ink away from a sharp pen line, because the pen point has cut the surface and broken through to the absorbent layer beneath.

• Check out the whiteness of your paper or board by putting a dab of process white or correction fluid on it.

• If you are doing a color cartoon for reproduction, the printer may need to wrap your artwork on a revolving drum for scanning. Do the cartoon on thin, flexible cardboard or "stripping board," a thick art board that can have the top layer stripped off for scanning.

• Most artwork is only done on board to prevent it from being folded or damaged in some way. If you wrap and reinforce packages well when you send them, then the artwork can be on as flimsy a surface as you like. If you work with a ballpoint pen on wax paper and the result looks fine, it is fine.

Paper and board

A smooth, non-porous surface; the ink dries on top rather than sinking in. You can create some interesting effects by scratching back the dried ink.

Paper

There are two surface qualities: hot-pressed, which is smooth, and cold-pressed, which is coarser and more grainy. Both are good for pen drawing, color washes, and gouache painting.

Art boards
Boards for illustration and graphic work come in a variety of thicknesses and finishes, with compressed surfaces or top layers that can be stripped. Line boards are smooth and perfectly receptive to ink; illustration boards have surface finishes comparable to the range of watercolor papers.

Tracing paper
This is useful for roughs, so you can build up your image with overlays, but is not so good for finished artwork.

Layout paper
A semitransparent, fine-grained white paper for layouts, which is very handy around the studio. You can use it for roughs, marker drawings, and color tests (but not for painting) and, since it is translucent, you can work from one rough or layout to the next stage by tracing over.

Drawing paper
This is not recommended for painted or heavily rendered work, but is fine for brush-drawings and sketching. There are slight differences in thicknesses, according to brand; double-weight drawing paper is heavy, resilient, and very smooth.

Acetate
Clear, hard plastic sheet used when an overlay is necessary; for example, when the lettering in comic strips may be translated for foreign editions and so should not be part of the actual artwork. Acetate is expensive – use it only if you really need it.

Drawing aids

Apart from the media you use for drawing and finishing artwork, several other items are useful or essential.

Erasers
The commonest, most available eraser is made of rubber. This type is not very efficient on a shiny or very smooth surface and best used where only a little cleaning is needed, as a lot of graphite will just smear. Never use the hard kind called "ink erasers," which spoil the drawing surface.

Plastic erasers are also easily available and are much more effective than rubber on line board and smooth (hot-pressed) papers. However, they can lift some ink from brush or pen lines if used too enthusiastically. Artgum erasers are, as the name suggests, suitable for art papers with a rough surface and for loose materials such as charcoal or soft pencil.

A kneaded eraser is difficult to get used to, because the material changes shape as you rub. But it is invaluable in that it doesn't attack the paper

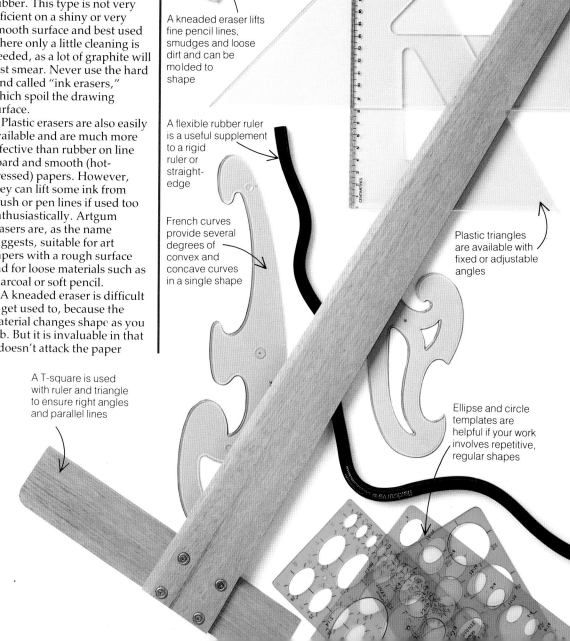

Plastic erasers are smooth, efficient, and clean for general correction

A kneaded eraser lifts fine pencil lines, smudges and loose dirt and can be molded to shape

A flexible rubber ruler is a useful supplement to a rigid ruler or straight-edge

French curves provide several degrees of convex and concave curves in a single shape

Plastic triangles are available with fixed or adjustable angles

Ellipse and circle templates are helpful if your work involves repetitive, regular shapes

A T-square is used with ruler and triangle to ensure right angles and parallel lines

surface at all, but simply absorbs the excess graphite. It is not as efficient at cleaning as, say, a plastic eraser and not recommended for clearing large areas, but is excellent for anything delicate; its kneadability means you can mold it into a thinner shape for extra care and precision.

There are electric erasers, best regarded as specialized and acquired only if you feel the ordinary types are not answering your needs. These are said to remove ink as easily as pencil, and can be used as a drawing implement to create smoky, faded effects.

If a large area has to be erased, start from a clean part of your drawing and work systematically through the graphite. If you smear the black across the surface, it can be very hard to get rid of.

Rulers
Avoid wooden rulers (they tend to be inaccurate); a transparent plastic ruler is a big advantage. Have one marked with American and metric measurements, down to ¹⁄₁₆in and individual millimeters. An 18in or 20in ruler is better than something shorter, since with triangles you also have short straight edges for fine ruling.

You need a beveled edge and a metal edge. The bevel is for ruling in ink, when it is best not to have the ruler flat on the paper as ink can puddle underneath. The metal edge – either a separate steel rule or a metal strip inset in a plastic one – is for cutting. Ruling with a blade against plastic inevitably results in slicing slivers out of the side, rendering the straight edge unreliable. Note that a steel rule may have been stored in a thin protective coating of oil, so make sure you clean it thoroughly before starting work.

Triangles
The most important part of the triangle for the cartoonist is its right angle. An accurately squared-up drawing is essential if your artwork has a border, as in a comic strip. You do not have to keep both 45 and 60 degree triangles – a single one will do – but you can alternatively invest in an adjustable triangle, which gives you all the angles you will need.

T-square
If you have a simple drawing board with straight sides, a T-square is very useful for drawing parallel horizontal lines (drawing boards with "parallel motion" have a built-in T-square). You can use your triangles to get parallel lines crossing at right angles or more acutely in relation to a fixed horizontal. A traditional hardwood T-square is more durable and practical than a plastic one.

Templates
The most famous and valuable template for drafting is the French curve, which has several convex and concave curves on its outer edges, and some ellipse templates (ovals) within the shape. You can buy one all-purpose template or a "nest" of curves in various sizes. The curve is very handy for drawing a curved line in ink when the need for accuracy overrides the desire for freshness and spontaneity in freehand drawing.

A slightly less versatile but useful item for drawing curves is the flexible rule. This is a strip of rubber that can be bent into curves and stays in the configuration until you change the shape again.

Other templates you may need are circles and ellipses. When a perfect circle is small enough to be too fiddly for compass drawing, a circle template is just what you need. Ellipse templates are similar, and excellent for drawing symmetrical curves on, for example, the top of a bowl or a dinner plate. These shapes are also preferred by some cartoonists for their word balloons (drawn after the lettering is complete, not before). Ellipse and circle templates made for professional drafting studios can be very expensive, but they are an investment for life. There are also less costly versions with fewer grades and sizes of ellipse.

Customized studio equipment
If you can set up a dedicated work space, this gives you a professional sense of what you hope to achieve, but specially made studio equipment is costly and can be acquired gradually as you see what you need.

An adjustable chair with supportive back is preferable if you are spending long hours developing ideas and concentrating on finished work

Parallel motion attached to the drawing board is useful for ruling borders, strips, and frames

Choose a work table or desk of a height that enables you to reach your work comfortably, without stretching or slouching

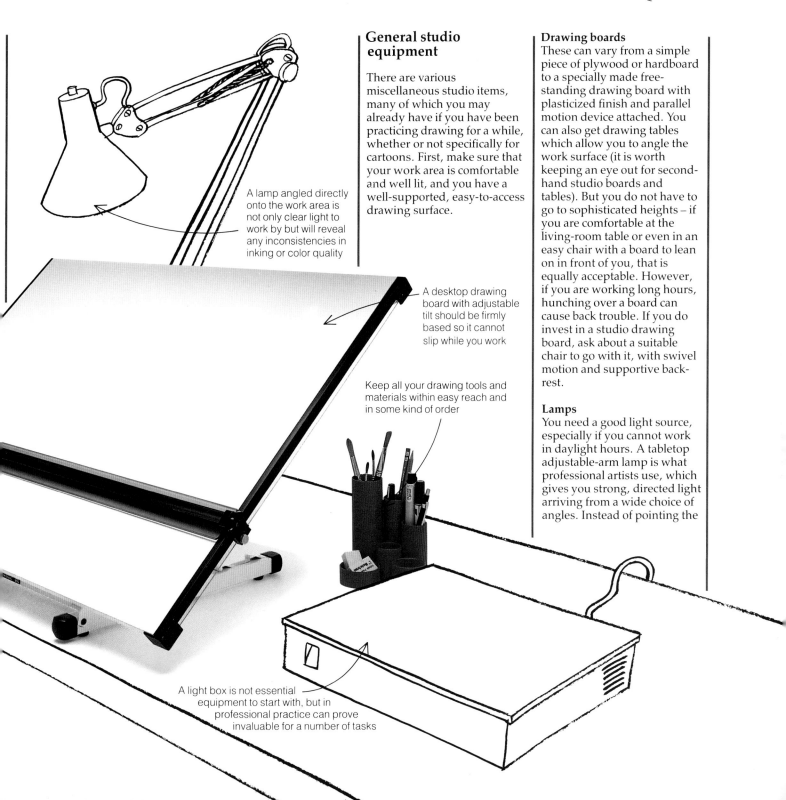

A lamp angled directly onto the work area is not only clear light to work by but will reveal any inconsistencies in inking or color quality

General studio equipment

There are various miscellaneous studio items, many of which you may already have if you have been practicing drawing for a while, whether or not specifically for cartoons. First, make sure that your work area is comfortable and well lit, and you have a well-supported, easy-to-access drawing surface.

A desktop drawing board with adjustable tilt should be firmly based so it cannot slip while you work

Keep all your drawing tools and materials within easy reach and in some kind of order

A light box is not essential equipment to start with, but in professional practice can prove invaluable for a number of tasks

Drawing boards

These can vary from a simple piece of plywood or hardboard to a specially made free-standing drawing board with plasticized finish and parallel motion device attached. You can also get drawing tables which allow you to angle the work surface (it is worth keeping an eye out for second-hand studio boards and tables). But you do not have to go to sophisticated heights – if you are comfortable at the living-room table or even in an easy chair with a board to lean on in front of you, that is equally acceptable. However, if you are working long hours, hunching over a board can cause back trouble. If you do invest in a studio drawing board, ask about a suitable chair to go with it, with swivel motion and supportive back-rest.

Lamps

You need a good light source, especially if you cannot work in daylight hours. A tabletop adjustable-arm lamp is what professional artists use, which gives you strong, directed light arriving from a wide choice of angles. Instead of pointing the lamp directly at the work, you may find it easier on the eye to bounce the light off a white wall nearby. The slight diffusion makes the light less harsh and the work less tiring.

An ordinary bedside light is usable, and you can get "daylight" lamps to fit. Regular light bulbs give off a slightly yellow glow, so color work that looks satisfactory by that light may appear very different in daylight. If your work is to be reproduced, bear in mind that a process camera sees the colors in conditions much more like daylight.

If you have fluorescent lighting in your workroom, an individual lamp may only be necessary if cast shadows are a problem in the immediate work area.

Light box

A light box is simply a lit screen that enables you to see through opaque paper and originals to trace elements from a drawing or reference image, or rework details to be collaged into the artwork. Light boxes are relatively expensive, but a good investment; sizes range from 8½ x 11in tabletop boxes to large studio light tables. For occasional work of this kind, however, you can use a window with the daylight as your light source; it is just not very convenient to draw against a vertical surface.

If you need to trace from a sensitive drawing, you will find that a dark photocopy provides a better line or tone to read through normally non-translucent paper or thin board; this is because photocopy toner is more opaque than graphite. You can also use a light box to work from a messy, sketchy rough and trace off a finished version directly in ink.

Knife

You will need a sharp knife for a number of jobs – always use a knife in preference to scissors. Unless you are doing heavy-duty cutting on thick board, an excise or frisket knife is the ideal tool. Handles and packs of blades are generally available from art suppliers. The most useful blades are the angled straight edge for cutting and a curved edge for scraping. Always keep plenty of fresh blades in stock – dull ones just waste your time.

If you do need to cut through heavy board, buy a sturdy craft knife with disposable or interchangeable blades. If your work regularly involves cutting complex, irregular edges and curves, a knife with a swivel-head might be an advantage. This is not cheap, so consider it only if you feel it might save you time and aggravation.

Cutting mat

This is useful though not essential – the back of a drawing pad will do. But a mat is a good investment and you can obtain a translucent one for

A craft knife with disposable blade sections serves to sharpen pencils, cut paper and cardboard, or trim artwork

A frisket knife is more refined for delicate work such as cutting out image sections, trimming mechanical tints or ink-line corrections

HELP!

Process white, used by professional artists for covering up mistakes

General studio materials
The items shown here are general studio materials commonly used by designers and illustrators.

Specially made cutting mats are marked with grid lines for accurate measuring and trimming

cutting on a light box, a time-saving and efficient combination, especially if you are doing the layout as well as drawing the cartoons.

Process white
This thick, opaque, pure white medium is what professional artists use to cover up mistakes. You might think that a dense white paint such as gouache or poster white would do as well, or even typist's correction fluid, but process white is specially made to be camera-friendly. You can use the other materials, but this is better.

It does have a tendency to dry in the bottle. Don't throw it away if this happens, just add a small amount of clean water

and fasten the lid, leaving the paint to soften.

Blue pencil
The fact that the process camera is not very sensitive to blue can be used to advantage. When you need to mark something on your cartoon that is not part of the final drawing – the boundary of a tone, for example, or an optional border – a light blue pencil (or marker) can be thought of as invisible. Blue pencil is also called non-copy pencil, and blue leads are available for mechanical pencils. But check with your publisher that this is suitable before you use it.

Adhesives
For pasting down patches, mounting drawings on board, and for collage or paste-up, you need some kind of reliable adhesive. Rubber solution

adhesive is the traditional glue used in paste-up studios, although the convenience of spray adhesive has widely taken hold. The rubber type is more economical, though rather messy. For small-scale gluing, the little adhesive sticks readily available at stationery stores are perfectly adequate and easier to use than wet adhesives.

When you use a glue-stick, push it up only enough to show a tiny rim of adhesive above the plastic case. This prevents waste and you don't knock off large pieces that you don't need.

Tapes
Drafting tape is low-tack and does no damage to a drawing surface. Masking tape is usable in an emergency, but more likely to affect surface finish. Ordinary clear adhesive tapes are usually very sticky, so you

only get one chance to lay them down, and can reproduce as a yellow tone; the matte-finished, low-tack types reproduce better and can be written or drawn on, but the edges attract dirt that may show up in photographic copying.

Gummed paper tape is used only to stretch watercolor paper before laying color washes. Soak the paper in clean water and tape it to a board with strips of gummed tape along all sides. Paper expands slightly or dramatically when wet, depending on its weight and composition, but shrinks again as it dries, and the tapes ensure it stays flat. Once stretched, it will dry back to a flat, smooth surface every time it is wetted.

Rubber-solution adhesive is an economical choice for frequent paste-up work or patching

Low-tack adhesive tapes can be used to secure, mask, or repair artwork

A glue stick is handy if you only need to use adhesive occasionally

ANIMALS

Animals feature in cartoons in two ways. Often they are a kind of prop or gag-feed for a human subject – someone riding a horse or an elephant, or talking to a dog or cat. But they can also be the subject of the cartoon, the character that the viewer identifies with, like Snoopy the dog, Garfield the cat, or the megastar Mickey Mouse.

These two functions also tend to indicate ways of presenting animals. When they are secondary players they usually appear animal-like, though their shapes and movements are simplified and characteristic features are exaggerated. Used as main subjects, they are more likely to be anthropomorphized: four-legged creatures are made to stand up on their hind legs and use their forelegs and paws like human arms and hands; their faces have humanized expressions of pleasure, terror, rage, or craftiness; they may even have clothes, shoes, and other such accessories.

To draw a cartoon animal convincingly, however much you simplify or distort it, you need to have a clear sense of how it looks and moves realistically so that you can interpret the shapes. You

should also be thinking about how the kind of animal you choose assists your "storyline"; with an elephant, for example, the fact that it is huge and lumbering is often part of the joke, but a cat can be weird and fuzzy or superior and sleek, so what is it expected to contribute to your cartoon?

A key aspect of simplifying an animal, especially in a strip where it has to move and be seen from various angles, is to use simple modular shapes which you can easily reorganize into different relationships. These are typically circles, ovals, and cylinders; the more complex musculature and joints are reduced to fluid lines and curves. To create a tense or aggressive character, convert to angular shapes. Scaly or folded skin, raggedy ears, and spiky fur or whiskers can be superimposed on basic forms.

FURTHER INFORMATION

Body Language, pages 38–39
Devices, pages 58–59
Figures, pages 68–71
Movement, pages 92–95

Simplification

If you have trouble drawing an animal face, take a simple face and draw around it the animal's most dominant feature, such as the lion's mane or the cat's whiskers.

Basic components

On this page, a dog's body is broken down into modular parts. This exercise involves building a mental picture of the dog like a three-dimensional construction that can be viewed from any angle. Once the basic components are assembled, they can be combined and recombined to make a repertoire of active and expressive figures.

◄ In the three-quarters view, standing, the neck is hidden behind the head.

▼ Altering the angles of the torso shape and the legs produces the begging posture.

▲ Sitting: the hindquarters rest between the hind legs.

▼ The body of the dog constructed using simple modular shapes. The main body is a horizontally angled, curved cylinder, or bean shape.

▲ The front view presents the basic forms in cross-section: the bean-shaped torso becomes a circle.

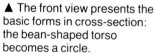

▲ The turned body combines the front view (far left) and the three-quarters view (top left).

◄ The upright legs balance the tilted torso as the neck and head reach toward food.

▼ Unbalanced legs as the dog performs a leap.

Anthropomorphism

The modular shapes of the dog shown on the previous page are no longer restricted to a purely canine form. Through engaging in human activities the animal figure becomes anthropomorphic, with the body erect and sitting on a seat instead of crouching. The dog's hind legs become human feet and its forepaws, like hands, can grasp things. The shapes of its head take on the features of the human face. The animal figure expresses human gesture and may wear human clothes.

◄ Playing a saxophone involves a human distortion of the anthropomorphic head.

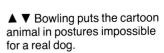
▲ ▼ Bowling puts the cartoon animal in postures impossible for a real dog.

▲ Anthropomorphism becomes more comic in direct ratio to the "humanness" of the activity, such as when the cartoon animal wears glasses to read.

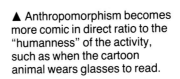
◄ Skating makes the canine cartoon figure balance as the human, with forelegs extended as arms.

Man into animal

▲ Just as an animal can assume human form, a few extra touches can make a human into any animal you choose. Here the rounded ears and circle at the tip of the nose have created an instant teddy bear.

▲ Consider how you might portray the running man as an animal, perhaps by changing the feet to paws.

▲ The addition of ears, nose, and tail complete the illusion. The hands are sufficiently generalized to be read as paws.

▲ Use the dominant characteristics of the animal you want to portray, in this case the long snout and thick, fleshy tail of the alligator.

Woman into animal

▲ Here the transformation from female human to teddy bear has involved changing the clothes as well as adding ears and turning feet into paws.

▲ For the more "feminine" form of the cat, the feet have been reinstated and a slinky striped skirt chosen.

▲ To turn girl into cow, the wings of the bow have become horns and the feet have spread into hooves. A nice touch of humor is provided by the hands holding out the skirt, as though in amazement at the unusual attire.

Fur and feathers, scales and skin

Animals have very distinctive markings. These don't have to be accurate but you can use them to identify your character.

Solid black tiger stripes

Fine horizontal lines for the hide of a rhino

Solid black for a rooster's comb

Scribbled line for a grizzled bear

Overlapping semicircles for fish scales

The patches of a giraffe: solid black on white

Animal expressions

Just use your imagination and the cartoon forms of an animal's face can express all human emotions.

Hilarity

Resentment

Bliss

Puzzlement

Duplicity

Smug

Frustration

Shock

Embarrassment

Variations on facial expressions

Classically, an upturned mouth denotes happiness and a downturned one ill-temper or gloom. See if you can create some variations of your own.

Angry   Shocked   Puzzled

Sorrowful   Laughing   Tired but contented   Happily exhausted

Gesture and movement

Body language is as important as facial expression in telling the story. Gestures such as hunching the shoulders or placing a hand on the chin can convey both emotions and thought processes.

Hatching a clever idea

Serious second thoughts   Disaster and panic

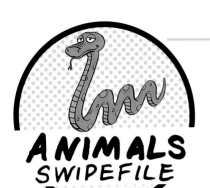

ANIMALS
SWIPEFILE

This swipefile contains a range of images by different cartoonists for you to copy or adapt. Use it to help you to explore ideas about style, technique, and characterization.

Thick fur is shown by broadly drybrushed outlines

Bristly fur and whiskers are drawn with short, even pen strokes

▲ A simple drawing but a relatively naturalistic bear – note that the powerful mass of head and shoulders is definitive.

▲ This rat's stance is heavily anthropomorphized; nose in air and arms on hips give him an arrogant, invincible manner.

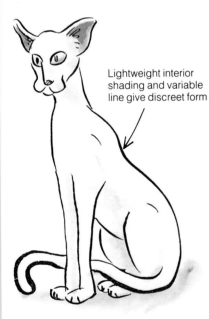

Lightweight interior shading and variable line give discreet form

Subtle line work and clear color washes complement the character's sophisticated style

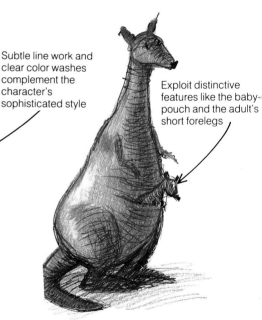

Exploit distinctive features like the baby-pouch and the adult's short forelegs

▲ Recognizably a real cat shape, but simplified to the point of being not quite real for cartoon purposes.

▲ Clothing a humanized cartoon animal is not unusual, but this one has the works – eyeglasses, cigarette holder, and medallion make him a stereotype of a stereotype.

▲ A kangaroo is pear-shaped and like no other animal, so it works in virtual silhouette.

Different line qualities show different fur textures on ears, face, and body

Emphasize any outstanding feature, like this elongated snout

▼ Few real snakes have a head angled abruptly to the body, but this is standard in cartoon snakes to add character.

▲ Some animals hardly need much input from the cartoonist – the shape of an anteater is funny on its own and gets a friendly treatment here.

Color and pattern can be a wacky version based on some idea of naturalism

▲ Animal caricature, making the most of the long lop-ears and the goofy teeth.

Solid blacks create a direct negative balance to white shapes

Tiny, loose strokes in black and color give life to the huge bloodshot eyes

▲ This drawing takes a fairly realistic view of the barrel-shaped body and slender legs, but the horse's face has a more-than-animal expression in its sinuous lines and big blue, long-lashed eyes.

▲ Swift, spiky brush drawing, breaking the lines on the jagged shapes, economically captures the startled movement of the bird.

▲ Animating the normally non-animate produces a tiny monster in this goggling clam.

▲ Seals are cartoon favorites, providing a lot of simple but telling detail.

31

BACKGROUNDS

There are several important questions you need to ask yourself about the background to your cartoon. Does it represent the real world, a stereotype, or a fantasy? Should it be there at all; if so, how much of it do you want to show? Is it just placing your characters in context, or providing a stage on which some kind of action occurs?

The actual size of your cartoon may restrict how generous you can be about background detail. Bearing in mind that you want to set the scene rapidly, simple indications may be sufficient – a horizon line, a couple of perspective lines, or a loose patch of tone or texture. Basic perspective elements show where people are in relation to their surroundings, and can help to place them in a large or small space, firmly on the ground or precariously high up in the air. Simple perspective makes sense of a scene, whereas if you try to fake it, the idea can collapse.

Stereotypical settings bring in all sorts of associations; the same characters are given different stories by the descriptive nature of the background, such as two men in a desert with an oasis in the distance, or the same two men in a narrow prison cell. Occasionally, the background is all that is visible, with a word balloon coming in to comment on the situation.

Narrative

It is possible to convey mood partially by applying light or color to your characters in a telling way, but a well-drawn background does much more. An interior or exterior furnished with suitable props can add a narrative background to the cartoon story, as well as a physical one, suggesting a whole way of life or a temporary crisis situation. The background is usually a stage setting for the characters, but can sometimes have a role in its own right, such as a storm, flood, or tidal wave.

If your background is a famous place, you don't have to use all of it; certain features are instantly recognized by readers familiar with the location – the dome of the White House, or the railings and gates of Buckingham Palace. Buildings are difficult, unless you have a flair for architectural drawing. Technically, it is easiest to use photographs, and copy or trace in line the features you need. But for all kinds of backgrounds you need to be able to draw the overall situation and its props; the key to this is good observation. Once you get into the habit of using your sketchbook, you will find that drawing backgrounds and background details becomes second nature, and you can soon spot the essential details that will make your drawing work. For unfamiliar or exotic settings, keep a file of magazine clippings.

FURTHER INFORMATION

Perspective, pages 98–101
Stereotypes, pages 108–109

Building a background

The purpose of a background is to show your reader when or where your characters are. Graphically, this means drawing the surfaces that surround a figure in order to convey all the information necessary for a gag. Treat the background as if it were built from the figure outward, gradually shaped around your character. This is illustrated as a stage-by-stage process in the series of drawings right, below, and immediately opposite.

▲ Ground the floating figure on a horizontal surface. A simple horizon line is enough.

▲ Show that your horizontal ground is not empty. Make it an environment: break the horizontal with a vertical line.

▲ Distinguish the environment – turn it into a location. Use pictorial details and props to define time and place as precisely, or as vaguely, as necessary.

▲ Dramatize the drawing. Render areas of black or graduated tone to add weight, solidity, depth or mood.

Reference material
Photographs are the most frequently used sources of reference for cartoonists. Below are two principal ways of using them for background architecture.

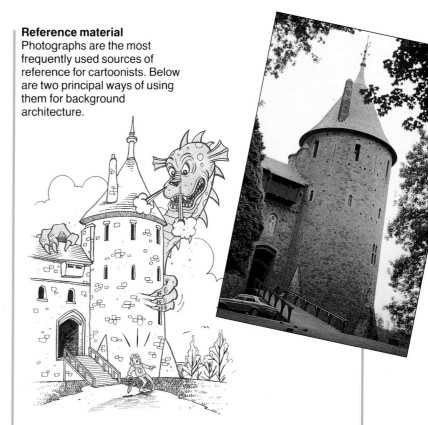

▲ Reference is used as picture: the shape of the castle and the viewpoint of the photograph are transferred directly. There are minor changes, but the important difference is in how the cartoon image is rendered.

▼ Reference is used as information: a preconceived cartoon image takes minor incidental detail of the Empire State Building from the photograph of Manhattan's skyline.

Telling the story

Once you have built up the background graphically, you need to consider what you want it to tell the reader about the characters you might place in it. Details of place and location also provide information on who the characters might be and what they might be doing. The pictures on these two pages show the same two figures, first in blank space and then against a series of five different backgrounds. In the first picture, all the reader can know about the characters is that they are female and male, young, and dressed casually.

The figures are put against a tropical background. Their presence together on an idyllic, vacation-brochure, deserted beach hints at a possible vacation romance.

The scene is an urban street. The silhouetted skyline suggests evening, and from the absence of cars or other people we could assume it to be Sunday. The two characters are looking around as they cross the street, which they would be unlikely to do in a city unless they were visitors. Thus the background makes these figures look like a young couple away from home in a kids-in-the-big-city cartoon.

This indoor setting could be any time of year, as the TV studio lights would be hot enough to permit the wearing of light clothing. The difference between the dress of the foreground figures and that of the program presenters in the background distinguishes the former as members of the audience – perhaps game-show contestants.

The positioning of the two figures at the top of the airplane gangway is a clear signal that they have arrived at a destination, again in a warm climate. Their outward glances could be the fascinated reaction of tourists to an unfamiliar place, while the plainness of their clothing suggests that they might be backpackers.

Here again, the background and clothing of the figures combine to explain who and where they may be. They could be students in a college library, but since they are in the Travel section it is more likely that they are planning a vacation.

The background story

In these three cartoons, the background gradually alters the point of the gag. In the first, the window cleaner is in a bad enough position, having lost control of his ladder. The background detail looks like residential houses, suggesting he is two or three floors up.

In the second cartoon, the change of background to the simply drawn but unmistakable high-rise buildings makes his predicament all the worse.

Finally, the "background" becomes a second character in the cartoon, giving the scene a completely different context. The way the huge ape brandishes the tiny ladder revises the viewer's sense of scale. Without background buildings, we can't assess how far the man is from the ground, but that is no longer such an important feature of the storyline.

BACKGROUNDS
SWIPEFILE

This swipefile contains a range of images by different cartoonists for you to copy or adapt. Use it to help you to explore ideas about style, technique, and characterization.

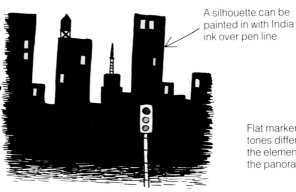

A silhouette can be painted in with India ink over pen line

▲ A city skyline can be rendered as line or silhouette according to how dark your image needs to be. Ask yourself: is it day or night?

Flat marker tones differentiate the elements of the panorama

▲ When drawing a landscape you must decide your illustration requirements. Do you need to show a specific place or a generic scene?

Earth-color washes for the interior background convey grime

▲ Backgrounds can also be stereotypes. This one is the setting for urban existential angst and decay.

▲ A generic shoreline shows the essential components of the meeting of land and sea. Figures and props can be added to suggest a specific type of location.

Compressed perspective produces a claustrophobic sense of space

▲ An uptown city street. Add props, such as street lamps, mail boxes, fire hydrants, or foreground people, to make a specific scene.

▲ The classic desert landscape complete with cactus, vultures, and burning sun.

Autumnal gold, brown, and purple are applied in thick pencil strokes

▲ Some backgrounds are subject to seasonal change. Use them to indicate time as well as place.

◀ The iconographic background is the setting for well-known images and motifs — in this case, of space exploration and space fantasy.

Working over the line drawing with colored pencils allows the color to carry atmosphere

▲ The size of the car interior, its exaggerated perspectives, and non-naturalistic colors all spell menace for the solitary little girl.

▲ This generic suburban street scene contains both stereotypical and typical elements.

BODY LANGUAGE

Cartoonists can pack a lot of information into a single image destined to be hastily scanned. As in the real world, body language can help to make a point directly, or supply additional, less obvious but enriching layers of meaning.

Posture illustrates personality and a character's relationships with the wider world. Timid or depressed people shrink inward; confident and aggressive people expand outward. Sympathy and attraction are expressed by people leaning or gesturing toward each other; antipathy and shyness can be shown by pulling away. The balance of the body is indicative of such states, with or without overt gestures.

Many gestures have become classic cartoon conventions, and they are broadly based on observations of how people actually behave. An overbearing character may be shown grasping or pointing, to pin people down and emphasize that orders are being given. People portrayed as embarrassed or slow-witted may scratch their head or fiddle with their ear – aimless gestures that show they are out of their depth. Surprise and joy are expressed as much by outgoing hand and arm

gestures as by the expression on the face. Gestures are typically complementary to facial expressions, although you can create an interesting tension by opposing the language of body and face.

Reactions are often highly exaggerated in cartoons – someone jumps up in the air when surprised, or falls flat with shock. There is an overblown drama in cartoon messages, and body language often takes a kind of pantomime form.

FURTHER INFORMATION

Figures, pages 68–71

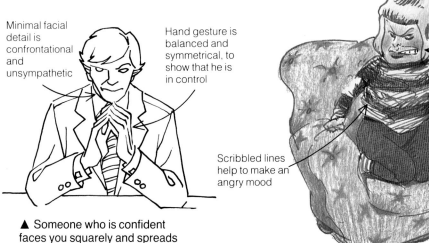

Minimal facial detail is confrontational and unsympathetic

Hand gesture is balanced and symmetrical, to show that he is in control

▲ Someone who is confident faces you squarely and spreads out sideways, presenting an impenetrable barrier.

Facial expression makes the rage explicit

Scribbled lines help to make an angry mood

▲ Anger could turn this armchair into a launching pad at any moment.

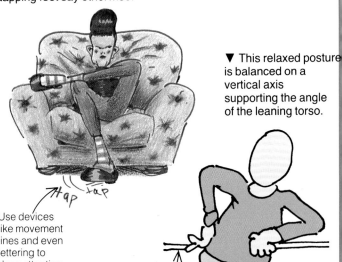

▼ Leaning so far back into the chair, this person could be quite relaxed, but the face and tapping foot say otherwise.

Use devices like movement lines and even lettering to draw attention to important indicators

▼ This relaxed posture is balanced on a vertical axis supporting the angle of the leaning torso.

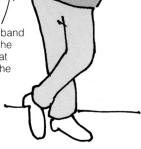

A simple horizontal band indicates the surface that supports the pose

The eyes look at nothing in particular, as if waiting for something worth seeing

The pressure of head on hands pushes up the soft flesh of the face

▲ Chin in hands, head slumped on shoulders, is a classic bored posture.

Disheveled hair and wrinkled brow show desperation

Clasped hands are very simply portrayed in block shapes

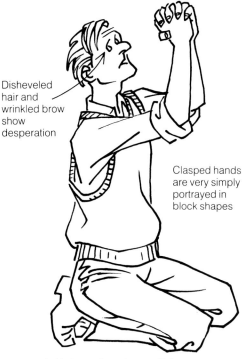

▲ Unless given to practicing a personal form of yoga, this man is obviously begging to be given a break.

The one alert eye reinforces the ambiguity of the pose – he's sizing up the situation

Clothing creases have a real basis but the lines visually add to the tension

▲ The upper body says "don't touch me," but the spread feet and forward tilt of the body suggest aggression.

▲ Anxiety or indecision may be the message of the hunched-in body and the upraised hand.

The shock of hair, fragile wobble lines, and exploding marks are all fear devices

◄ The crossed-arm comforting gesture shows horror here, not depression, and the bent legs leap away from a sudden terror.

The character's own shoulder acts as something to hide behind

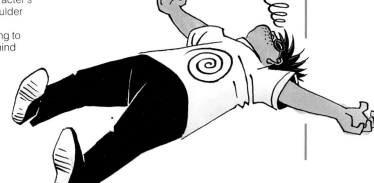

BRUSH DRAWING

A lot of people find drawing with a brush much more difficult than using a pen or pencil. That is because in ordinary writing and drawing, we make small-scale hand and wrist movements, while with brushwork you need to get used to drawing with your whole arm, letting the brush travel freely on the paper.

Start by experimenting with the kinds of marks you can make. You will find that the smoothness of thick lines you can draw with a brush is very useful for emphasis. You can get subtle thick-and-thin variation, especially around angles and curves, increasing your range of line qualities.

If your image includes elements with a lot of body, such as tree trunks or furniture, a brush helps give some weight to the drawing. And for putting heavy shading on a scene a brush is the ideal tool. The physical properties of a brush are also very useful for particular tasks; for example, drawing a person with shiny hair. You can achieve very fine lines flowing into a highlight area, and the texture of the brush is naturally sympathetic to the subject.

It is important to be aware of which areas of your drawing are wet, and which are dry. If you are drawing direct or inking over a pencil rough, work downward through the image to avoid moving across ink that is still wet. It isn't convenient to have to turn the board around when you are trying to draw recognizable forms with some consistency.

FURTHER INFORMATION

Light & Shade, pages 86–87
Line Qualities, pages 90–91

Fine drybrushing

An old brush is best for this technique. Load it with ink and blot off the excess, then stub the brush on paper to splay the hairs, and stroke it gently over the paper to make fine, multi-stroke lines.

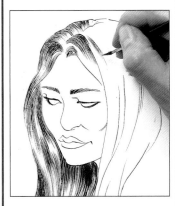

▲ The shiny texture of the hair depends on a lot of highlighting. As you apply the brushstrokes, vary the density of tones to make the texture flow. Fade down into the highlight areas, then brush up from below, leaving the whites clean.

Feathering

This technique is used to shade organic shapes, making a broken texture along the lines where forms interlock.

▶ **1** Do not overload the brush, the strokes should be fluid, quick and light. Build up a kind of directional hatching with a solid black edge for darkest shadow.

▼ **2** The forms are built up with strokes of varying lengths and weights, according to the detail of the musculature. White highlight areas are preserved to form contrast.

Coarse drybrushing

The artist is looking for a contrast of line qualities, using fluid strokes to draw the lion face which will contrast with the rougher texture of the drybrushed mane.

1 The brush is blotted to remove excess ink before the zigzag lines of the mane are drawn. The ink starts to run out quickly, making a fuzzy, dragged texture.

2 The finished drawing treats the animal head as relatively simple shapes, but the varying qualities of the brush drawing express different features of the subject.

Light, shade, and texture

▼ Consider three different brush renderings of the same scene. From each, a detail is enlarged and inset for close study of the particular qualities of each brush technique.

▲ This treatment includes much fine detail, such as the tiny brushstrokes rendering silhouetted pine foliage in the background. The fire and the figure's features are more naturalistic, even to the point of resembling Elvis Presley.

▲ Dry brush is used to render the effect of light from the fire as it casts shadows that reveal the ridged and graveled surface of the earth.

▲ The shadows in this scene are feathered strokes, brushed out of dark areas in the direction of the light. The detail reveals reflected light on rocks around the fire's base, rendered by strokes radiating away from the firelight out of shadow lines on each rock.

▲ The cartoon face reduces human physiognomy to a set of abstract features, rendered without shadow by simple dots and strokes of the brush.

◀ The cartoon rendering aims at expression. The figure and fire are mainly outlines and the area of light around both is a uniform ellipse.

41

This branch of cartooning is basically about drawing real people, though you can caricature a type. The viewer has to be given enough recognition factors to identify the person and understand the joke. The subject doesn't have to be world-famous, but must be sufficiently well-known in the context in which the cartoon representation appears, so it could be a schoolteacher or family member. Some people have a natural feel for this, but some expert cartoonists find caricature impossible because it involves portraiture, the need to obtain a likeness, however distorted.

A caricature can be a face or a whole figure. The image is developed by homing in on a particular feature, or more than one, that is absolutely characteristic of the person physically, and may also seem to say something about his or her personality. Large noses or ears are very useful, full lips or small eyes, an exaggerated hairstyle, or a distinctive shape to the face, such as a pear shape either way up. If you are drawing the whole figure, the person's posture can be a key factor – a very upright, stiffly held body, or one that is stooped or bent. Mannered gestures are also valuable ammunition in a caricature.

Familiar characteristics

When a person is exceptionally famous, or stays around long enough to become completely familiar to a wide range of people, the caricature can be honed and reduced to the bare essentials. British Prime Minister Margaret Thatcher, for example, became little more than a particular configuration of hair, nose, and chin in some representations over the years. Some well-known people present a special challenge because they are relatively unremarkable physically. Among US Presidents, Bill Clinton is less easily caricatured than Ronald Reagan, because his features are more even.

The easiest way to develop a caricature is to work with a medium you feel comfortable with – pen or pencil – and just sketch and doodle, gradually pulling out important features until you get a stereotype of your subject. An alternative method is to use photocopies of snapshots or newspaper pictures and trace over parts of them or collage them together. If you have access to an enlarging photocopier, you can rearrange the proportions of the face quite quickly this way, and it is helpful if you are not confident of your drawing.

FURTHER INFORMATION

Faces, pages 62–65
Figures, pages 68–71
Hands, pages 76–79

1

2

3

Development of a caricature
Illustrates the development of a caricature from photographic reference through finished drawing. Most caricaturists use some if not all of these stages.

1 Although you can draw caricatures from life, a photograph will supply details which may not be remembered or which would be otherwise unavailable.
2 Pencil an outline of your caricature, blocking in its general shapes. This is an important stage; if a likeness is not achieved early on, the finished drawing may prove unsatisfactory.
3 Draw in the finer details, developing the characteristic features of dress, body shape, and facial structure.

4

5

4 The pencil drawing is traced onto a smooth line board for an ink rendering of the rough. Here a strong, variable line is needed both to define the shapes of the caricature and to fill in shadows and other solid black areas. If your caricature is intended for reproduction at a small size, this may be as much detail as you need.

5 To finish the drawing, tone is applied by cross-hatching, using a fine, rigid pen. At this stage, photo reference can help again to make detail of light and shade convincing. Also, a highlit edge to the figure increases the appearance of roundness.

Exaggeration
▼ A very effective caricature. By exaggerating the subject's long face, much narrowed, and heavy, hooded eyes, the artist creates a sense of weightiness that also emphasizes the drooping posture.

Mechanical aids
▲ This artwork is pieced together from photocopies enlarged to different sizes, with ink and process white used to cover joins.

Changing proportions
▼ This is an attractive portrait, swelling the proportions of the face to focus on the broad smile and laughing eyes.

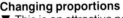

Celebrity caricatures
When you are drawing well-known people, you can not only look for the outstanding physical features but often also make use of actions or props particularly associated with the person and what they do.

◀ The famous face, crinkly hair, and skinny body are only half of Michael Jackson's persona. The fact that his stage clothes are often a kind of uniform gives the artist an extra identification feature, and his robotic dancing style is unmistakable.

▶ Fred Astaire's pointy nose and long chin lend themselves perfectly to caricature. The exuberant dance movement expresses both profession and personality. Simple, solid black shapes are appropriate for the rather formal clothing.

◀ The archetypal cowboy John Wayne, caricatured at a period beyond his prime, when the formerly craggy features have softened and rounded. The artist has done a good job of overlaying hatched shading on the circling lines of the face without destroying the form.

In a lot of cartooning, economy is essential. When drawing clothes, you cannot capture all the detail, so you need to ask yourself what it is you want to convey. Is the clothing loose, does it hang from the body? Is it stretched, showing the form underneath, like leggings or a snug T-shirt? Is it important to show that the clothing is stiff and starchy, or an item that keeps its own shape?

Another aspect of clothing in cartoons is for signaling the type of person you are portraying. Figure out simple codes; for example, the basic shape and features of a business suit. You need not include a lot of accurate detail – you are basically looking for an unambiguous, "shorthand" description. On the other hand, some telling detail adds to effective characterization – for a bag-person, the clothes may appear dirty and uncomfortable; someone very rich may have a lot of jewelry and accessories. Clothes can very directly indicate social status.

The shapes of clothing and the ways they relate to the body can provide a lot of information about implied movement, especially in a comic strip where the image changes from frame to frame.

Here it is helpful if you have kept things simple, so you can easily work out how the clothes would stretch or drape differently as your character changes position.

FURTHER INFORMATION

Figures, pages 68–71
Stereotypes, pages 108–109

◄▼ When you are using simple line work, concentrate on the shapes of the clothing and any accessories or pattern detail that emphasize the character, like the little girl's cute bow, short skirt and ankle socks (left) or the chef's traditional stripy garments (below).

◄ Scribbled fiber-tip line wraps the clothing around the body. The colored pencil work emphasizes the way the clothes just form an outer skin to the body shape.

▲ In this sequence the shading and patterns are important to the movement. Watch how folds follow the bend and stretch until the accordion effect of the upside-down pose. The flared pants emphasize direction in leg and foot movements, and their stripes widen over the lit curves and narrow into the shaded folds.

▲ Baggy, casual clothing hangs loosely from the body. The watercolor wash adds to the casual feel.

◄ Shapes and colors help to build a personality. This person's clothes are bright and slightly wacky, giving her a simple charm.

CLOTHES SWIPEFILE

This swipefile contains a range of images by different cartoonists for you to copy or adapt. Use it to help you to explore ideas about style, technique, and characterization.

▶ Baseball cap and mobile phone specifically accessorize a basic teenage dress code.

Denim fabric conveyed economically

◀ This style-victim has it all wrong – the clothes don't fit and his shirt is wrinkled and stained. Clumsy shoes complete a picture of fashion disorientation.

▼ Whatever shape this woman has is lost in her sturdy coat, given one continuous all-around curve by the plaid pattern.

▲ An old-time cowboy typically wears a checked shirt and baggy, rumpled chaps.

▶ Comfortable clothes, as all the smoothly drawn lines and shapes suggest. The pattern is inessential but livens up the drawing.

The cartoonist has conveyed a bulky, heavy fabric

The matching hat doubles as a pet dog

▶ A Supergirl lookalike has the basics right – color co-ordinated with underpants outside her tights – but is she steady enough on those heels to save the world?

48

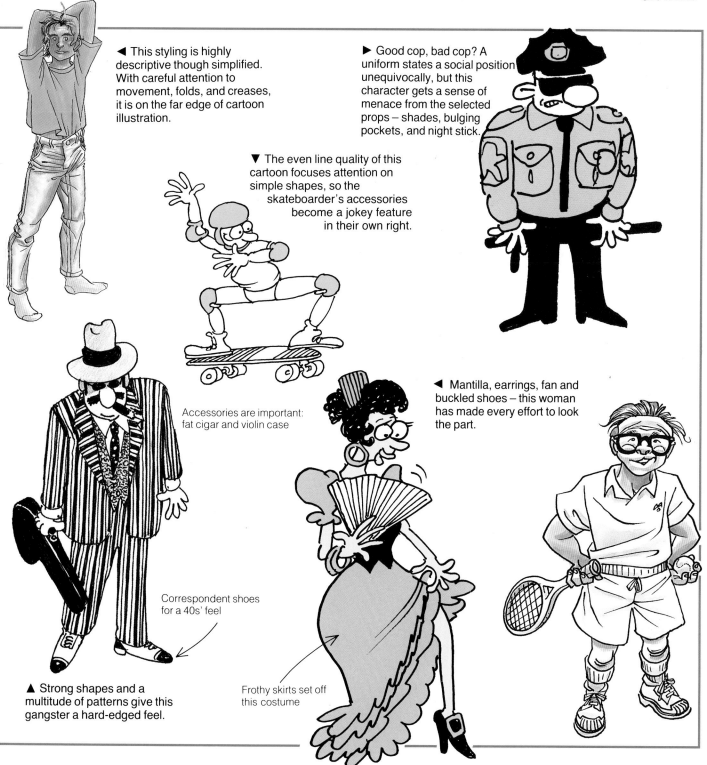

◄ This styling is highly descriptive though simplified. With careful attention to movement, folds, and creases, it is on the far edge of cartoon illustration.

► Good cop, bad cop? A uniform states a social position unequivocally, but this character gets a sense of menace from the selected props – shades, bulging pockets, and night stick.

▼ The even line quality of this cartoon focuses attention on simple shapes, so the skateboarder's accessories become a jokey feature in their own right.

Accessories are important: fat cigar and violin case

◄ Mantilla, earrings, fan and buckled shoes – this woman has made every effort to look the part.

Correspondent shoes for a 40s' feel

▲ Strong shapes and a multitude of patterns give this gangster a hard-edged feel.

Frothy skirts set off this costume

Color can be one of the best ways to emphasize the message of your cartoon. It is obviously a more expensive option at every stage – a/w, film, plate making, and printing so it is not always within budget. There are two basic considerations for the cartoonist: the aesthetic understanding of how to use color and the practicalities of telling the printer what you want.

Aesthetics

If you have the luxury of using color in a cartoon, the question you need to ask is whether it basically acts as decoration for a drawing or is a functional element of the image. If the color works fully as a descriptive element, you do not have to put a lot of line work down before you start working with your color medium. Decorative color, on the other hand, needs a strong linear structure; the black-and-white drawing should work perfectly in its own right, and the color is extra.

Colors have two basic properties – chroma, which is the brightness and intensity of the hue, and tone or tonal value, which is the degree of lightness or darkness. You can make use of these properties, and the visual relationships between different colors, to give sparkle and definition to your cartoon. There are elements of color theory that you can learn and use deliberately, but you also acquire an understanding of color through practice.

Practicalities

Spot color is, simply put, one color in addition to black and white. It is usually flat color or

The color wheel

The color wheel arranges the three primary colors – red, yellow, and blue – in sequence with the secondary colors – orange, green, violet – mixed from primary pairs, and intermediary shades. Colors opposite each other on the wheel, such as red and green, are called complementary; they contrast intensely. Colors in adjacent segments, on the other hand, make harmonious relationships.

As well as complementary contrast, you can make use of the contrast of warm and cool colors.

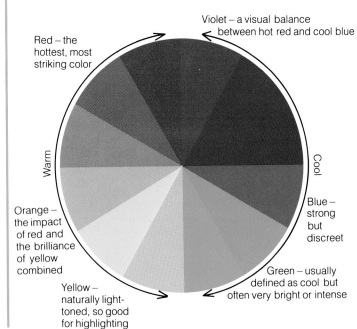

Red – the hottest, most striking color

Violet – a visual balance between hot red and cool blue

Warm

Cool

Orange – the impact of red and the brilliance of yellow combined

Blue – strong but discreet

Yellow – naturally light-toned, so good for highlighting

Green – usually defined as cool but often very bright or intense

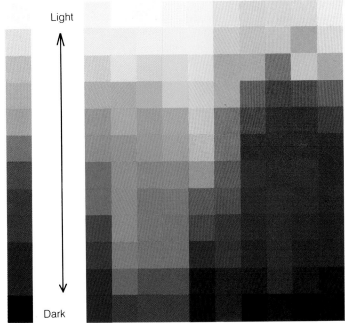

Light

Dark

Tonal contrasts

▲ This shows the breakdown of the tonal variation applied to different colors. Clearly, each gradation of a single color provides contrast with gradations above and below it.

As with hue, you can make color harmonies between colors of similar tonal quality and saturation. A series of design handbooks is devoted to listing such combinations. Some artists use these for coloring their cartoons or strips.

a dot screen, intended to enliven the drawing or draw attention to focal points. Where you are able to use more than one color in a decorative role, it is often advisable to limit your palette; especially if the drawing is complicated, a small color range holds it together. Generally the spot or second color will be predetermined by the publisher or client as it needs to be the same throughout the publication.

To decide where and how to apply decorative color, take some photocopies of your drawing and try out color applications freely. You may lose a little spontaneity when you come to coloring the final image, but by planning in advance you avoid making errors that have to be covered up, which the camera may pick out again when the cartoon is reproduced. Watercolor is the ideal medium for applying decorative color directly, as it is transparent and does not obliterate the ink line.

The four-color reproduction process works by overprinting only four colors – magenta (red), cyan (blue), yellow, and black – as a series of tiny, even dots. The original image is photographically screened and dot-films are produced which break down every color and tonal variation into a percentage mix of process colors. If four-color printing is available to you, there is no limit to the color range and techniques that you can use, but this is the most expensive form of reproduction. Spot color is cheaper, as there is only one color film to be made.

The actual color does not have to be taken from the original; the artist can indicate the color areas as gray or non-repro blue tones and the printer puts them on to a color plate.

FURTHER INFORMATION

Line & Wash, pages 88–89

Limited color
When you have a limited color range, you can choose to make a cool harmony or a striking clash for impact.

▶ Yellow and violet are high-contrast complementaries, lit up with pure white. Orange tints relate to yellow. Two or three related colors with one complete opposite is a classic way of picking a dynamic color scheme.

▶ Green, blue and violet run in sequence on the color wheel and are cool colors, so the combination is restrained and attractive. Violet only on the figure makes him stand out.

▲ In this flat-colored, schematic arrangement, there is no shading to give depth, so the contrast of warm and cool does the job.

Dramatic contrast
Putting color to work in your cartoons means dividing your drawing into harmonizing and contrasting fields of temperature and tone.

▶ A combination of warm/cool and low/high intensity color in which the hues are also gradated to shade form and depth.

Color in print

There are many ways to get from a piece of finished artwork to a printed color copy of your cartoon. None of them should affect how you invent your gags but each can influence the kind of artwork you produce and the way that you draw it.

In most cases, the method by which your artwork is reproduced will be the result of cost considerations, given where your cartoon is intended to appear.

Below and opposite, the principal methods of print reproduction are explained with examples using a simple black-and-white image of astronaut and goldfish bowl and applying different ways of preparing it for printing in color.

Single color

Solid black (100%)

▲▼ Printing a single color – usually black – is termed monochrome printing. Most newspapers and magazines contain monochrome sections which include cartoons. For these, you can draw line artwork, line and wash, or use percentage tints, as below.

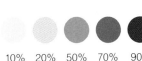

10%   20%   50%   70%   90%

Two or three colors

Black   Special color

▲ Printing two or three colors usually involves printing black plus one or two extra colors.

▲ You can choose spot colors from the extensive ranges of inks available as solid colors.

Four colors

Cyan   Magenta   Yellow   Black

▲▼ In the four-color process, you produce full-color artwork which is separated electronically into an image made of magenta, cyan, yellow, and black dots.

Specifying color reproduction

▲ A simple line drawing is marked with non-reproducing blue, invisible when scanned, to indicate a tint area.

▲ The printed image shows the line drawing with a tint area inserted photographically, following the areas of blue on the original artwork.

▲ In order that you don't have to touch your original artwork, you can attach an overlay and mark color on it as a quick guide for the origination house.

▲ In print, the image follows the areas of color indicated on the photocopy. However, where hand-separated color is used, most color appears flat, like a patchwork quilt.

▲ A common method in preparing your line artwork for color is a "mark-up" on overlays with color areas blocked in and percentage tints specified.

▲ Marking up allows you fairly tight control over the placing and density of spot color, or your choice of extra colors, when your cartoon is commissioned for two- or three-color printing.

Laying color tints

▼ A tint can be a single color, or a combination of inks. Spot color is the most widespread use of tints for cartoonists. Unlike the four-color process, this only allows a limited choice of colored tones. Two colors is defined as black and a spot color.

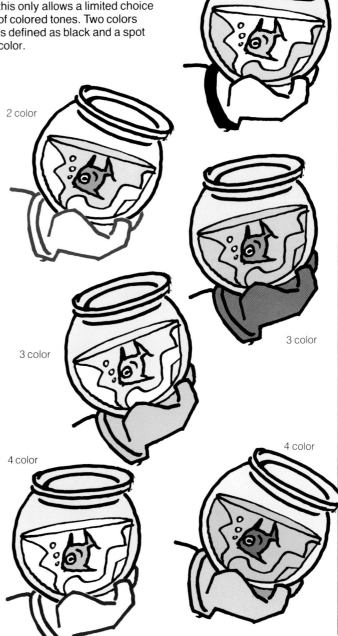

3 color

2 color

3 color

3 color

4 color

4 color

▲ Full-color artwork is the most widespread method of producing color cartoons for publication, even though this means reproduction via the expensive four-color process.

▲ Four-color reproduction enables printing from the whole range of chromatic and tonal variation. The disadvantage is that solid blacks can sometimes look patchy.

COLOR SWIPEFILE

This swipefile contains a range of images by different cartoonists for you to copy or adapt. Use it to help you to explore ideas about style, technique, and characterization.

▼ Use color for clarity. Here objects are differentiated by filling the white areas of a black-and-white image.

The natural fade of a sky is reversed to heighten contrast with the foreground tree

▶ A comment on unhealthy lifestyle – the man's grayed coloring makes it obvious that a diet of burgers (attended by flies) is doing him no good at all.

The red tongue makes a horrid, greedy focal point in the gray face

Bright-colored, dripping relishes are based in reality but over-lush

▼ Here the envious green is inserted in a picture otherwise colored quite naturalistically, emphasizing the "storyline."

Red/green complementary contrast increases focus on face

Clothing colors and shading stick to a limited range of red, blue, gray

▲ Local color is used in this image, but selectively. By leaving a background white, you can focus attention on what is essential for a gag.

► This relatively detailed color drawing uses the contrast of opposites – red and green – to create pattern interest and highlighting.

Cold blue-green highlighting on black is as effective as white

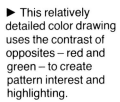

Pale-toned yellow highlights the sharp shapes of eyes and beak

► Dark colors can be relied on to add malevolence. The artist has graded rich blues into the black ink washes.

▼ Solid red always tends to zoom out of a picture, and is particularly dynamic on black, but the yellow trail leads the eye back to the home planet.

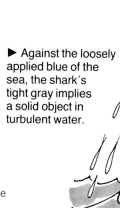

◄ Bright primary colors, contrasted with the muted umber of the boat and paddle, draw the eye to the panicked figure of the boatman.

► Against the loosely applied blue of the sea, the shark's tight gray implies a solid object in turbulent water.

To give the rocket maximum force, background shapes are in cool, muted blues and grays

CORRECTIONS

You have a few options for correcting your work when something goes wrong – erase or scrape it off, cover it, patch it. The appropriate technique depends on what medium you are using and the area of the artwork that needs correction.

Erasing pencil is relatively easy; ink, especially waterproof ink, is relatively difficult. Be careful not to do anything that damages the paper surface so much that you cannot redraw cleanly. If you are working in ink on a very smooth surface, you may be able to scratch back the line with a frisket knife. This is a useful technique for refining line qualities and eliminating small errors, but unsuitable for erasing large areas.

Correction fluid isn't usually pure white, so be careful if you use a cover-up method on color artwork. Process white is an opaque medium that is invisible to the process camera – use it in preference to typist's correction fluid or white gouache.

Patching can be done in one of two ways. Either you can stick a clean patch of paper over the particular section of your drawing and ink onto it (let the adhesive dry before you start; damp paper may tear or spread the ink line). Or you can cut out a patch around the error and stick the fresh paper to the back of your artwork. The second method is better if you are doing a large correction; sometimes you need to rework up to half of the drawing. On inked artwork, it is ideal if you can arrange the patch to fit into an existing outline, which conceals the cut edges.

To disguise a patch – the camera may pick up a cast shadow from the edge of a stuck-on section – smooth down the edge with your fingernail, then "puddle" some process white along the join to soften it.

Using process white

▲ Small errors where ink has smeared out from the line are easy to cover. Make sure the ink is completely dry before brushing undiluted process white evenly over the smudge, working carefully up to the line.

Patching from above

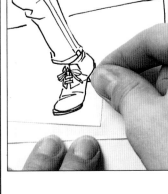

▲ 1 This method can be used to correct part of a drawing. Cut a piece of paper slightly larger than the area to be corrected, stick it over the artwork, and redraw the detail in pencil before inking the lines in style with the rest.

▶ 2 Flatten the hard edges of the paper patch by running your thumbnail along them firmly.

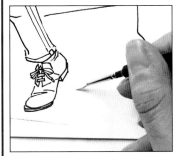

▲ 3 Load a brush with process white and brush it thickly across the smoothed edge to "fill" the join. Do not brush along the edge, work at right angles to it.

▶ 4 In this image, the artist has successfully added shoes to a figure that was originally barefoot. The correction will not show up at all in a line reproduction.

Cutting away a background

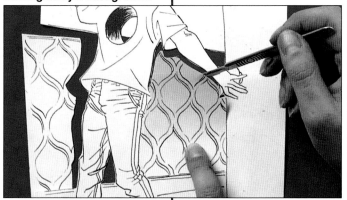

▲ **1** To alter a large area of your drawing, such as a whole background, it is easiest to cut out the good part of the drawing and stick it to a clean ground. Use a very sharp frisket knife blade and cut around the shapes just outside the ink line.

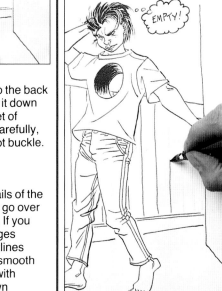

▲ **2** Apply adhesive to the back of the drawing and lay it down evenly on a fresh sheet of paper. Smooth it out carefully, making sure it does not buckle.

▶ **3** Pencil in the details of the new background, then go over them with pen and ink. If you think any of the cut edges around the original outlines show up too strongly, smooth them down and paint with process white as shown opposite.

Scratching back

▲ **1** This technique can be used on a smooth-surfaced line board or paper. The artist has penciled and inked this drawing, but decides to change the shape of one hand.

▲ **2** A curved frisket blade is scraped lightly along the dried ink lines. You can see that tiny curls lift from the paper surface with the ink; do not press too hard. The corrected shape is penciled in and then inked. The technique is not suited to fibrous drawing papers as the surface will break up and spread the ink.

Cartoons have a large number of conventions that act as a sort of shorthand for conveying actions, noises, or states of mind. They are part of the comedy of exaggeration, giving larger-than-life qualities to ordinary subjects or making things visible that are not physically present in static, soundless scenes.

One of the best-known and most obvious devices is speed lines, trailing out from people's feet when they are running, or from car or bicycle wheels. There are variations on this visually – sometimes the speed is shown just by straight lines, which give a whizzing effect; you can also use little puffs of smoke, suggesting that the character is burning up the road by running so fast; to show that a long distance has been covered, the lines might meander broadly to add the extra length within the shallow pictorial space.

Other devices include short, sharp lines coming out of a dog's mouth to indicate an ear-splitting bark, and huge beads of sweat breaking from a face on which the features are also drawn exaggeratedly to convey enormous anxiety or effort. The sweating is disproportionate – you don't normally see great droplets flying off anxious

people – and that is part of the gag. Exploding sound effects of the Wham! Zap! type work the same way. By contrast, the light bulb going on over somebody's head to show a great idea suddenly dawning is associative rather than exaggerated.

These examples are all too familiar, and we have learned to read them the right way. There is room for some new ideas of your own, but the visual impact has to be immediate and obvious, so that the device enhances the overall mood or message of the cartoon rather than distracting from it.

FURTHER INFORMATION

Lettering, pages 84–85
Movement, pages 92–95

Sounds
Cartoons use lots of visual equivalents for sounds. Think about the quality of the sound and what kind of line or shape can interpret it.

Curving lines are "sweet," and music has its own symbols

This chick is still learning and its song is shrill and jagged

Lines that fan out suggest increasing volume; straight lines are hard, direct sounds

A one-note whistle swells out in a cloud of air – give it some momentum with speed lines

Burst bubbles are a standard device to indicate a drunken or dazed state of mind

Movement lines do not always show speed – this is a slow, weaving path

The double line on the shoe soles gives him an unstable base

▲ Drunks and drunkenness
Drunkenness has a whole range of devices relating to the person's physical state and actions. Start with the overall body language, like this drunk's free but unsteady movement.

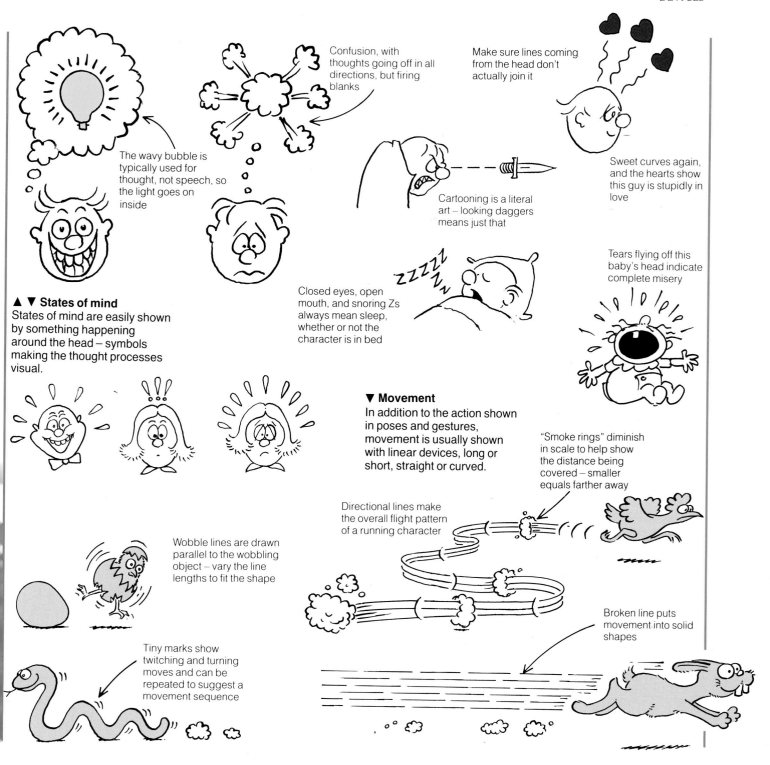

The wavy bubble is typically used for thought, not speech, so the light goes on inside

Confusion, with thoughts going off in all directions, but firing blanks

Make sure lines coming from the head don't actually join it

Sweet curves again, and the hearts show this guy is stupidly in love

Cartooning is a literal art – looking daggers means just that

Tears flying off this baby's head indicate complete misery

▲ ▼ States of mind
States of mind are easily shown by something happening around the head – symbols making the thought processes visual.

Closed eyes, open mouth, and snoring Zs always mean sleep, whether or not the character is in bed

▼ Movement
In addition to the action shown in poses and gestures, movement is usually shown with linear devices, long or short, straight or curved.

"Smoke rings" diminish in scale to help show the distance being covered – smaller equals farther away

Directional lines make the overall flight pattern of a running character

Wobble lines are drawn parallel to the wobbling object – vary the line lengths to fit the shape

Broken line puts movement into solid shapes

Tiny marks show twitching and turning moves and can be repeated to suggest a movement sequence

EXPRESSIVE DRAWING

Distortion and simplification are the cartoonist's bread and butter. Often the cartoon is a tiny melodrama in which exaggerated or dramatic features help to put across the point quickly and with the greatest impact. One means of achieving this is to emphasize specific attributes of your characters, so that they become, in effect, cartoonist's caricatures, though not necessarily of known persons. In action pictures you can distort bodies and use abrupt foreshortening to convey mood and movement. Or you might borrow the visual effects of other artistic styles, such as that of the European Expressionists, who used the bold drama of black and white in dynamically stylized woodcuts and drawings.

The composition of your drawing can also be contrived to make the overall scene more expressive. Harsh angles and directional lines suggest power and aggression; curves and concentric shapes have a calming effect, although this can also be sinister, say, if an anxious or agitated cartoon character is isolated within a serene background. In fact, a sugar-coated world in which everything and everyone seems perfect and happy is as much of a distortion as a purposely disturbing rendering, because the artist has abandoned the truth.

Expressive drawing is about adjusting the facts to suit your story, or the type of world and its inhabitants that you want to convey. You can begin with real detail from your sketchbook and decide which way you want to take it.

FURTHER INFORMATION

Devices, pages 58–59
Movement, pages 92–95

Emotional transformation
A transformation from slight discomfiture, implied by the raised eyebrow, to shock-haired, open-mouthed, fanged raving. Thinking about the face as a spectrum of expression in this way enables you to consider what is most appropriate in your cartoon.

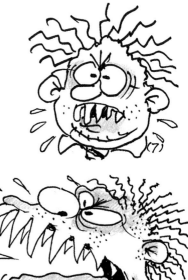

▲ These cartoons include two different reactions to the same situation. Top, unexpressive drawing. Above, on the way to manic raving.

▲ A little girl complains when her father buys the wrong ice cream. In the top drawing, there is restrained reaction, needing a verbal gag to make it funny. The humor in the drawing above is entirely visual.

Bodily transformation
Simple technique expresses straightforward character – the line work conveys nothing remarkable about this guy.

The outline here is more variable, with broken line and downward shading in the torso emphasizing the limp, somewhat anxious posture.

The line quality here flows and curls, echoing the melting shapes, and this is complemented by soft charcoal tones replacing the more dynamic style of hatched shading. Color sets a mood – blue is the color of sadness and depression.

FACES

Just as in life, where you watch a person's face for their response and mood, faces and heads are extremely important in cartoons and appear more than anything else when you are conveying a story. There are two specific tasks for the artist in this: the ability to draw a face convincingly (although not realistically), with proportions and features that make sense; and the ability to alter that face to convey particular expressions and actions – sadness, pleasure, pain, shouting, nodding.

Even though in cartooning you can simplify or exaggerate to a great degree, it helps to get the basic shape and proportions right. The schematic drawings shown here will help you to identify the position of features, and their relationships to each other. You then need to practice turning the head and face to different angles, with the arrangement of features following logically from the viewpoint selected.

Faces can be round, oval, squarish, pear-shaped. The shape can help to give your character an identity. Then there are details relating to sex and age. In comic strips, where the characters are often relatively realistic, women and children typically have less detail on their faces than men. Extra marks on the face tend to suggest the heavier musculature of males, so for women you have to find economical ways of showing, for example, crow's feet patterns and laughter lines.

With expressions, there are various useful conventions based on observation. Pleasure pulls the features upward, sadness pulls them down. Anxiety or fear is often conveyed by rounded shapes – starting eyes, open mouth. But there are subtle degrees of variation for expressions, even in the simplified language of cartoons. A teaching exercise we use consists of asking students to draw someone crying. When they have done that, we ask them to draw someone who is sad. Usually, they have used up all their ammunition on the first drawing, and have to think very hard about how else sadness can be conveyed.

FURTHER INFORMATION

Body Language, pages 38–39
Caricature, pages 42–45
Devices, pages 58–59

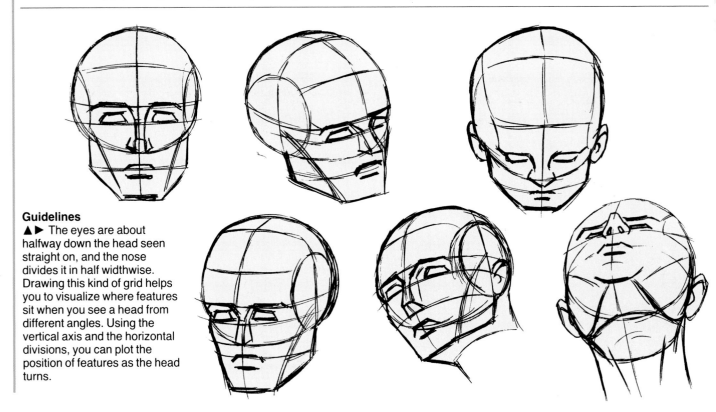

Guidelines
▲▶ The eyes are about halfway down the head seen straight on, and the nose divides it in half widthwise. Drawing this kind of grid helps you to visualize where features sit when you see a head from different angles. Using the vertical axis and the horizontal divisions, you can plot the position of features as the head turns.

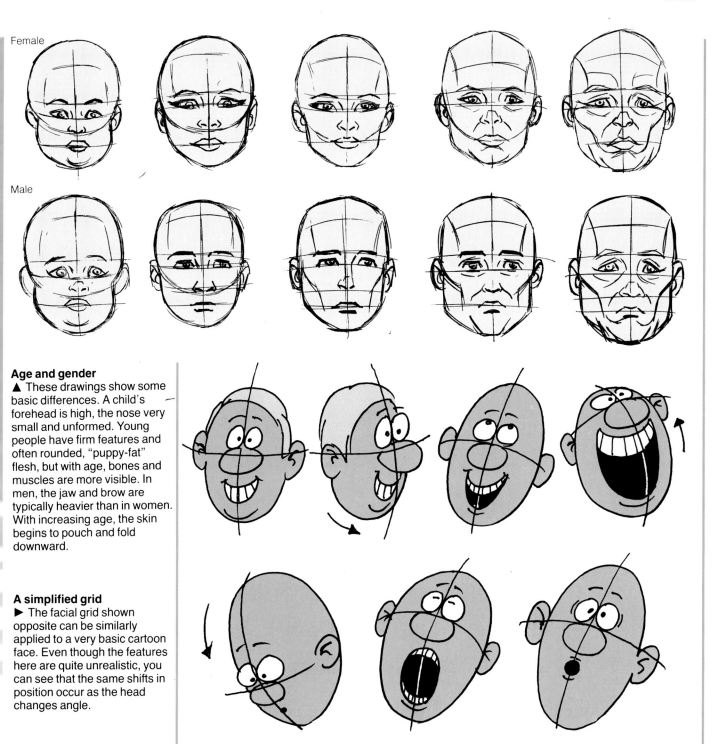

Female

Male

Age and gender
▲ These drawings show some basic differences. A child's forehead is high, the nose very small and unformed. Young people have firm features and often rounded, "puppy-fat" flesh, but with age, bones and muscles are more visible. In men, the jaw and brow are typically heavier than in women. With increasing age, the skin begins to pouch and fold downward.

A simplified grid
▶ The facial grid shown opposite can be similarly applied to a very basic cartoon face. Even though the features here are quite unrealistic, you can see that the same shifts in position occur as the head changes angle.

FACES
SWIPEFILE

This swipefile contains a range of images by different cartoonists for you to copy or adapt. Use it to help you to explore ideas about style, technique, and characterization.

Eyes are rounded in alarm

The solid black jagged outline of the hair emphasizes shock

▲ For extreme expressions, a realistic face can be drawn with exaggerated features.

▲ Expressions dominate in these felt-tip pen drawings, portraying (from top) nonchalance, rage, and insolence.

◄ The hand is essential in reading this drawing as a yawn. Without the hand it appears more like song.

▲ Eyes and mouth double as peaceful and sleeping expressions.

▲ Similarity of heads and faces mark this pair as a couple.

◄ This face is a support for props that describe the character – shape of glasses frames, hairstyle, even the style of shirt collar.

▲ Prominence of nose and lip fill out the features of a busybody.

► The bland face normalizes a deviant dress style.

► The turn of the head gives this impassive face a story to tell.

► This drawing makes use of contrast and shock tactics. The ugly, inelegant face contradicts the expectations raised by the dainty "feminine" styles of hair and costume.

► All the features are realistically positioned, but this face is deliberately elongated and unnaturalistically colored.

Feet are notoriously difficult to draw; even rigorous figure artists may fudge on the issue. It is not always the actual structure of the foot itself that causes problems, but the need to show feet standing firmly on the ground, forming the contact point between the figure and its surroundings.

Ideally, try to pick up a simple idea about how the foot is put together, as in the drawings here, then consider how you can articulate this in your own drawing, according to what the feet are doing. Feet can be fairly expressive and may become a sort of "sideways" gag in a cartoon; like hands, for example, the feet can be expressing something different from what the face seems to be saying.

Feet are commonly covered up by shoes. Here again, the shape and gravity relates to the shape and movement of the foot, though you can approximate.

FURTHER INFORMATION

Clothing, pages 46–49
Hands, pages 76–79

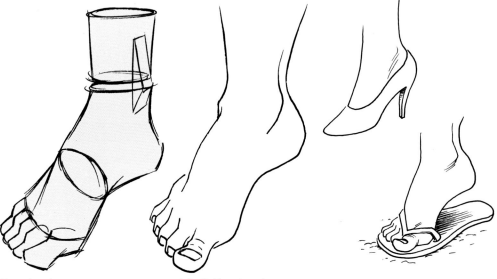

Drawing feet
▲ 1 Consider the foot as a set of modular parts, constructed to allow the body to balance upright on an even surface.

▲▶ 2 Rendered naturalistically, the stepping foot supports the balance of the body. The examples of footwear are designed to emulate both step and even surface.

▼ 3 Use the modular construction of the feet to think about how the articulation of their parts, seen from a variety of angles, can function expressively in your drawing.

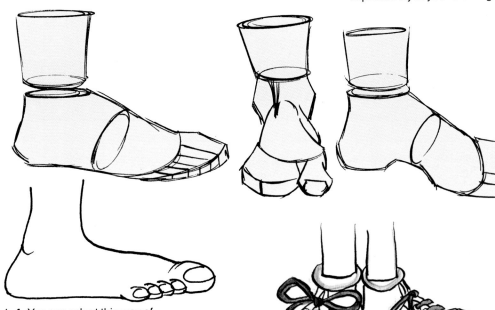

▲ 4 You can adapt this way of thinking about the construction of the foot to building the kind of exaggerated shape more suited to cartooning.

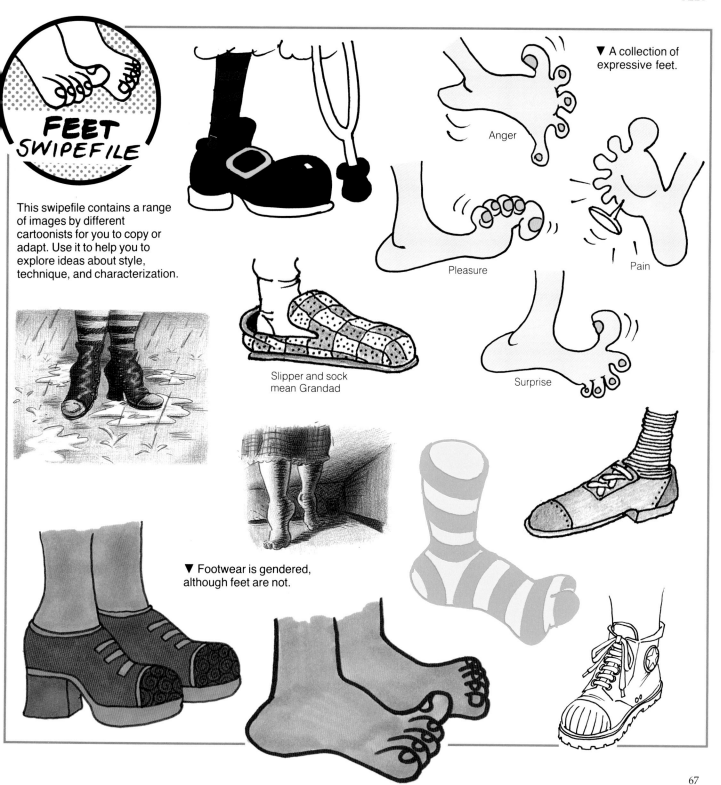

FEET SWIPEFILE

This swipefile contains a range of images by different cartoonists for you to copy or adapt. Use it to help you to explore ideas about style, technique, and characterization.

▼ A collection of expressive feet.

Anger

Pleasure

Pain

Surprise

Slipper and sock mean Grandad

▼ Footwear is gendered, although feet are not.

FIGURES

The human figure attracts the eye over and above any other subject in an image, because we naturally associate with the human element. So a quietly drawn figure doing nothing in the corner of your cartoon has the potential to become a focal point. Keep this in mind when you decide who should appear in your cartoon frame and what they are contributing.

If you find figures difficult to draw, here the conventions of cartooning are on your side, because you can, and perhaps should, simplify or distort. The basic proportions of the human figure are considered to be about 1:6–7 head to body length. A ratio of 1:4 gives you a more compact, dumpy person (but this is the correct proportion for children, whose heads are relatively large); a thin, tall, gawky person might be 1:8 or more. Be careful when you are including two or more people that their relative proportions have some sort of consistency, otherwise the drawing may seem incorrect and out of scale. Unless there is a comic reason to distort immensely, you need to preserve the relationship of body and limbs as well: whether a person is tall and stretched or wide and compact, their elbows and hands will approximately align with waist and mid-thigh respectively.

You can gather material by sketching people at home or on the street. Television, magazines, and other people's cartoons also give you useful information. Look for typical, obvious elements – short, tall; fat, thin; upright, stooped; young, old. The posture and apparent energy of a figure can say something about who the person is. Pay attention to clothes, hairstyles, and accessories; not only the detail of what people choose to wear, but how it relates to showing off or disguising their physical attributes.

The drama of a cartoon, especially comic strips, often depends upon foreshortened limbs or whole figures, exaggerated gestures, and implied movement. These complex subjects are treated under separate headings.

FURTHER INFORMATION

Body Language, pages 38–39
Clothing, pages 46–49
Faces, pages 62–65
Feet, pages 66–67
Focus, pages 72–73
Foreshortening, pages 74–75
Hands, pages 76–79
Movement, pages 92–95

Human proportions

Few human beings conform strictly to the standard proportions, but it is helpful to know how the "basic model" works, as this helps you to recognize and play up individual differences, as shown in the three drawings here (center right). You might, for example, want to exaggerate a key feature, such as a small head, big feet or particularly long legs. Bear in mind too the obvious differences between the male and female figure. The schematic drawing of a man shown here could be adapted to a woman by making the shoulders and waist narrower and the hips wider. The proportions of head to body are more or less the same, though women's heads tend to be smaller.

Body types

Even when much of a person's body is obscured by clothes you can convey the basic figure type. You may find it helpful to make schematic drawings.

▼ The thin, unmuscular body and narrow shoulders are stressed by the obvious weight of the shopping bags.

Over-large head and angle of neck emphasize narrowness of shoulders

Large feet contrast with bony ankles

▼ The most obvious difference in proportion between child and adult is the size of the head, which here has been deliberately exaggerated, as have the rounded eyes.

▼ A well-muscled body in loose clothing can sometimes appear simply fat, so choose revealing clothes such as T-shirts.

Short tight sleeve reveals bulging biceps

▼ Tight clothing – or minimal clothing such as a swimsuit – is a good choice when fatness is treated as the subject of caricature.

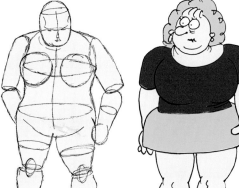

Short skirt and unsuitably pointed shoes make a point of the bulging legs

Aging

The human figure changes dramatically with the passage from babyhood to adulthood, the most noticeable difference being in the relative proportions of head and body. In late-middle and old age people alter in shape rather than proportion, either accumulating fat and spreading in certain areas or becoming stringy and skinny. Posture typically becomes more hunched, and flesh begins to sag, producing pouches and wrinkles.

The diaper proclaims this a baby, but equally so does the large head and rounded limbs.

The head is still large in proportion to the body, but more revealing are the posture and clothes – thumb in mouth and slipping shorts.

The plump child has become a thin, uncertain young man, with typical sloppy dress, awkward posture, and adolescent spots.

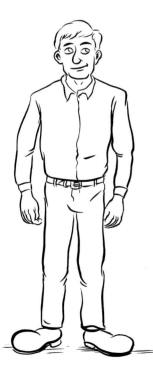

A reasonably fit, muscular, and broad-shouldered adult male, confident and ready to face the world.

Ten years later, the smile is still hopeful and the expression alert, but the beer-belly has become pronounced.

Life is less attractive now, and face and figure are beginning their drooping descent into old age.

The body has shrunk, making the feet and hands appear unnaturally large, and the head is no longer carried upright.

FIGURES SWIPEFILE

This swipefile contains a range of images by different cartoonists for you to copy or adapt. Use it to help you to explore ideas about style, technique, and characterization.

▼ An exaggerated walk conveys a showy character.

◄ The similar graphic treatment of these two figures stresses the physical similarity, suggesting mother and daughter.

▼ Successive layers of transparent ink model the weight, mass, and local color of this figure.

Skin and flesh highlights are reserved as white paper

A split brush renders the texture of coarse, swept-back hair

▼ The more realistic a figure is, the more care must be taken with the balance of gesture and posture.

Flat marker colors complement fine outline details

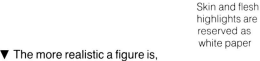

◄ A high overhead viewpoint produces complex foreshortening and tilting of the figure's angle, emphasizing the irritable movements of this waiting man.

▲ This "bigfoot" figure is identified as a mechanic through the use of costume and props – dungarees and a spanner behind the ear.

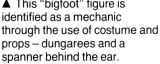

FOCUS

There are all sorts of ways in which you can direct your viewers to the point of the cartoon or lead them through a story, whether a single image or strip. Through the organization of the image you can ensure that a figure or object makes immediate impact, or you can spread the action more subtly and let the viewer realize gradually where the punchline comes in. However, attention span for cartoons is short; as a general rule, you don't want to complicate the means of communication. Even if you are going for a slow-fuse approach, you can allow only a couple of seconds for the point to come across.

Perspective gives you directions and angles relating to the actualities of the scene that can lead the eye toward the focal point of the cartoon. There are also simple diagrammatic divisions of a rectangle that naturally indicate where the focus will easily be picked up. This helps you to arrange the composition effectively and maintain a continuity through the image.

Alternative methods of creating emphasis are technical and visual – a thicker line quality, a splash of bright color, a dramatic value contrast. These are all based on creating one element that stands out from the rest, even having a more obviously three-dimensional quality. But don't overdo it – the emphatic part must remain integrated with the rest of the image, or some of your work will go unseen. If you knock down background elements too far, they may become obsolete (perhaps they are unnecessary), so think about the overall composition in these terms also.

FURTHER INFORMATION

Perspective, pages 98–101
Viewpoint, pages 122–123

Two types of focus
▲ On this page are two examples of focus in its simplest forms. Above, the picture is treated as if it were all on one plane: a two-dimensional field, divided into contrasting areas of tone. The central character is made the focus by leaving him without tone.

▲ Here, the central figure is isolated by linear, pictorial devices. Perspective lines from the edges of the room converge on the figure, relating its outline graphically to the edge of the field.

▼ The visual field is divided into simple areas of black and white related by the direction of hatching. This converges on the crystal ball, emphasized by the direction of the background figure's gaze.

▼ You can focus your reader's eye using color contrasts with great richness and complexity. Here, contrast moves focus between the bright, warm colors of the figure in the doorway and the second figure.

Focusing devices
▲ Use a bold line. Not only does the dog fill more of the visual field than the man, the thick contrasting lines of its face and forepaws, and the foreshortening of its figure, bring the dog into focus.

▲ The videotape is a solid black area within a white area which is, in turn, within another solid black. In the white area, the gaze of the figures combine with these divisions to signal the tape's importance.

Focus and depth of picture
The depth of an object in a picture determines how much space it occupies in the visual field. Below and right, examples show the same object at different depths.

Image and space
You can draw attention to an image not merely by how much of it fills a given image area but by how it fills the area. Below, a highly contrasted drawing of a shark breaks into the page via an area normally reserved for the white space of the margin. This device is usually reserved for use in strips.

Top right, the typewriter is the picture's focus. Above, the typewriter is an integral part of the background, although in focus, linked to the left figure. Right, the typewriter is relegated completely to the background; focus is entirely on foreground characters.

FORESHORTENING

This is an exaggerated perspective effect applied to figures and individual objects. Its value in cartooning mainly relates to making subjects seem to come at you from the page, which aids the melodramatic impact typical of cartoons and comic strips. The classic example is a figure with one arm flung out toward you – perhaps pointing, punching, or beckoning; in the drawing, the person's hand appears much larger than the head, and the receding perspective travels along the arm and shoulder. A similar effect is applied to, for example, a foot kicking out or a large running step, and the principle also applies to objects coming at you directly; say, in a strip, the nose-cone of a spaceship looming up.

This works on an illusion of things seeming near or far, although the actual distance between them may be relatively small. There is a subjective element to it, in which you can decide the relationships of scale and proportion for yourself depending on how exaggerated you want the illusion to be. But you can use basic perspective methods to plot the image. Decide how much of your field of vision is occupied by the nearest part of your subject, then fix a notional vanishing point and extend lines back toward it. Within this framework, the other elements of your subject are roughly fitted.

For a human arm stretching toward you, for example, you can interpret the shape as a simple cylinder. At the front is a large circle, at the back a tiny one, and the two are joined by straight lines gradually converging as they recede. The lines are a directional guide, not a fixed outline; you may want to flesh out the shape as a bulging, muscly arm or a wrinkled sleeve.

FURTHER INFORMATION

Movement, pages 92–95
Perspective, pages 98–101

Degrees of foreshortening
The drawings below show how the principles of perspective produce foreshortening in the shapes of a cylinder and a cartoon spaceship, seen from three angles of view.

▲ As the viewpoint shifts, the tops of both cylinder and spaceship appear larger, their bases are relatively small, and their lengths are increasingly truncated.

▶ The forms of the cylinder and the spaceship are dramatically foreshortened to measure about half of their length in side view.

▼ The side view displays the cylinder as a rectangle, with no curvature of volume. The spaceship is in cross section.

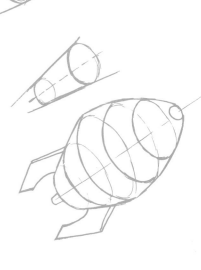

Foreshortening the figure

This follows the basic principle of near/large and far/small. This is easier if you break down the shapes into basic building blocks of spheres, ovoids, cylinders, and cubes.

▲ The hand held up in anger is a set of curved cylinders and ovoids. To draw the cartoon version, start with a close-up of the hand and draw back, showing smaller proportions, to give a 3-D effect.

Drama

▲ You can use foreshortening to accentuate the drama of cartoons, by stressing the depth of a picture. The foreground character's foreshortened arm runs through several depths of picture, combining the division between foreground and background with focusing devices.

◄ When you are foreshortening the child's figure, start with a very large sphere for the head. Even without foreshortening, children's heads and faces are drawn proportionately larger than adults'.

▶ Foreshortening makes the dramatic object the biggest in the drawing. The studded boot is the beginning of the drawing. The rest of the figure is drawn back from this in perspective.

After the face, hands are probably the most expressive part of the human anatomy. The face and one or both hands can often say a lot more than a whole figure. Hands form a limited, small-scale part of overall body language, but their gestures can give a much more specific context to the expression on the face.

As with all the most vital elements of cartooning, straightforward observation of your subject is the essential starting point. Study hands to see the proportions of fingers to the back and palm of the hand, look at the articulation of the joints – where the knuckles lie, where the thumb joins in. The hand is a very complicated and flexible piece of machinery, and the more you know about it, the more you can use it expressively. But with any kind of drawing that involves stylization, once you know the rules, you can break them. Some cartoonists show hands as minimal scribbles.

There are various cartoon clichés relating to hands – the beckoning hand, the fist, the open palm, the thumbs-up sign. Practice drawing these gestures until you get them down pat.

Cartooning also has a tradition of simplifying hands, borrowed from cartoon animation. They are shown with only three fingers, which makes them easier to draw and makes the shape less complicated or crowded in drawings that are typically quite small and intricate enough. This convention is often applied to cartoon animals, when their paws are converted to hands to anthropomorphize the creature. But whatever the reason, a hand with three fingers can point or make a fist as well as a four-fingered one. If you get the expressive element right, the reader probably won't notice that a finger is missing.

FURTHER INFORMATION

Body Language, pages 38–39
Faces, pages 62–65
Feet, pages 66–67

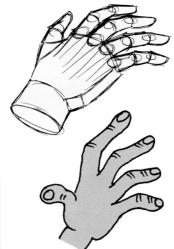

Basic shapes
If you think of a hand as being strictly segmented, like a robotic construction, it makes it easier to work out shapes and angles.

A hand held out flat, palm or back toward you, is relatively simple to define as a set of basic shapes.

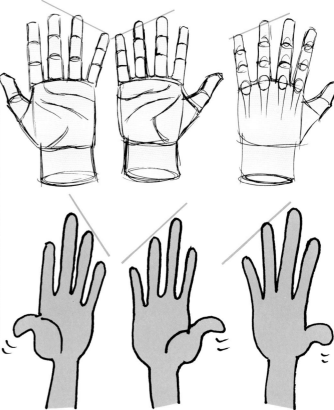

▲ In these simplified drawings the important factor is the movement of the thumb, indicated by speed lines. Only the absence of the thumb crease in the last drawing shows that this is the back of the hand.

◄ Hands can be deliberately distorted as long as you provide visual clues, in this case the fingernails and creases over the knuckles.

► A three-fingered hand can be as expressive as a five-fingered one, but if you use this kind of simplification it must be carried through the rest of the drawing.

Hand gestures

Hands are very expressive both in life and in illustrations, particularly when in contact with the face. As these examples show, simple but effective drawing solutions can be found in any style.

This gesture is more powerful than a single finger pointing but more ambiguous. The ink drawing technique gives it a tough texture.

In this firm "stop" gesture, the hand is given an exaggerated backward slope.

Hands holding objects

When you draw a hand holding something, look for the way the fingers curl around the object, and try to indicate how tightly or loosely it is held, however simple the shapes you are using to describe both.

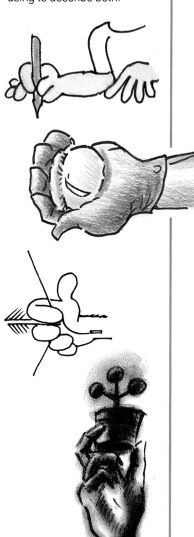

This is a tense and threatening gesture, expressed by the claw-like outer shape.

The sausage-shaped fingers are unrealistic, but the beckoning-finger gesture, reinforced by speed lines is easily understood.

One hand waving – and the wobble lines cheerfully provide the to-and-fro motion.

Hand and body gestures

"I can't stand it."

"Well, can't you get it back?"

"I'm telling you, just do it."

"How can this be happening?"

"I'll hang it up there."

"What did I do with it?"

HANDS SWIPEFILE

This swipefile contains a range of images by different cartoonists for you to copy or adapt. Use it to help you to explore ideas about style, technique, and characterization.

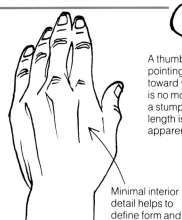

A thumb pointing toward you is no more than a stump, its length is not apparent

Minimal interior detail helps to define form and direction

▲ Even line weight is applied to an accurate outline, with angled fingers slightly foreshortened.

▲ An outflung hand has quite an odd shape, the palm becoming very wide but less deep.

Tight wrinkles show pressure within the curled fist

► This powerful, compact shape gains muscular weight from variable line partly shadowing the curves.

◄ When a hand is holding a pen or pencil, the main pressure is on the index finger.

Hand and gun work as parallel, interlocking shapes

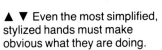

▲ Hands and fingers can be simplified; here the interlocking hands form a triangular shape.

Heavy shadowing helps to show direction in the fingers

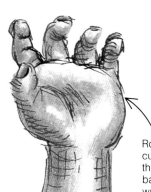

Rounded curves show the hand tipped back from the wrist

▲ A chubby hand has less flexibility; note the smooth curve of the palm toward the fingers.

▲ ▼ Even the most simplified, stylized hands must make obvious what they are doing.

Devices double the impact of a punch

▲ In different gestures by the same character, keep basic shapes and details consistent.

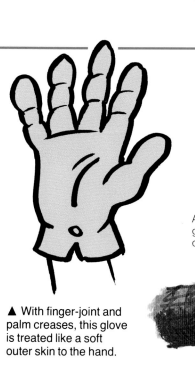

▲ With finger-joint and palm creases, this glove is treated like a soft outer skin to the hand.

A loose-fitting glove coarsens the outline shapes

A tight-fitting glove smooths out detail

▲ The bulk or fit of a glove determines the sensitivity of grip and movement.

▲ The pressure needed to rip the paper is made clear by the way the bottoms of the fingers bend outward.

▼ This flexed hand gains movement from sketchy line and shading in fine fiber-tip pen, with color wash giving form.

▲ If an object being held is important, make sure hands are arranged to show it off clearly.

▼ A pointing hand is easy to read and dynamic, however simplified.

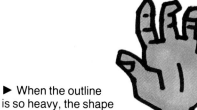

► When the outline is so heavy, the shape needs to be equally strong.

The bent finger is slightly out of scale to draw attention

A rather unnatural grip, again designed to show the whole object.

▲ A surprisingly delicate gesture from a simple, strong drawing.

This is a method of depicting shading that creates three-dimensionality and mood in a black-and-white drawing. Simply described, it means working in a series of parallel lines, traveling fairly evenly in one direction. Crosshatching is a "doubling" of the technique. Having put down a set of lines, you hatch over them more or less at right angles to intensify the value.

If this sounds somewhat rigid and graphic, it certainly doesn't have to be. Hatching and crosshatching can be orderly and regimented if desired, but the technique can also be used freely, with lines loosely scribbled and scratched. What you are aiming for is the impression of "gray" tone within a particular area, which may be raggedly finished or cleanly hard-edged. The black and white combination forms the effect of gray mid-tones; the depth of tone depends on how widely spaced are the lines and how heavy or fine.

Apart from being an expressive way of shading, this has the advantage of reproducing as line rather than halftone; it is essential to certain kinds of print production that you don't use solid grays. It works equally well in pencil or ink, though when a pencil drawing is reproduced as line only, some of the subtleties may be lost.

FURTHER INFORMATION

Light & Shade, pages 86–87
Stippling, pages 110–111

Types of hatching
The pictures on this page illustrate the different ways in which you can combine layers of hatching to create varied densities of tone. Below are details exemplifying each method, taken from the main picture, right.

▲ Hatching drawn in the direction of the light source renders the unlit side of a moon, with a secondary layer suggesting reflection.

▲ Crosshatching combines uniform strokes, overlaid at angles to produce a net-like balanced texture of lines.

▲ In multiple hatching, three or more layers of hatching create a dense texture where tone finally takes over from linearity.

▲ Curving, hatched lines signify direction of surfaces on terrain and boxes, notably on the moons.

▲ Crosshatching defines the direction and surfaces of boxes, along with foreground and background terrain. Multiple hatching is used to distinguish the bottom box of the pile from the crosshatched ground.

Hatching shapes and forms

You can kill a cartoon drawing with the wrong sort of hatching. The illustration plus details below and right show hatching as integral to the image.

▲ The mad nun's form is picked out by lines at right angles to lines radiating from the candle flame.

▲ Hatching follows facial contours and shadows.

▲ Lines fan out from the flame as tonal ground for the image.

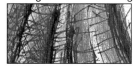

▲ Crosshatched drapery superimposes angled lines, to show the hang of the garment.

The direction of the lines in hatching is crucial. The image lives or dies according to whether a crosshatched cartoon shapes the object or merely makes a pattern.

▲ Contour lines following neck, chest, and facial features, impose a pattern of lines which also defines mass and volume.

▲ Uniform hatching adds simple tonal value to the hues which distinguish the parts of this image.

▲ Multiple hatched areas overlay hatching. Note limited contour hatching on cheeks, chest, and shoulders.

Hatching in context

▶ The mail car of a train is being robbed by stereotyped masked Western bandits. Hatching is used sparingly to differentiate parts of the picture by areas of tonal density and to hold the action at its center. However, the basic hatching types outlined on these pages are put to use here.

Short contour lines follow the curvature of the roof and the metal side of the car. The mail guards' uniforms are hatched by carefully drawn horizontal lines, contrasting with the short, angled strokes hatching the bags behind them. In the foreground below left, a horse's head is hatched in narrow horizontal lines, contrasting with the wider lines of the guard's uniform.

Cartoon ideas can come from anywhere: something catches your attention or makes you laugh, and seems worth a visual comment. But it is hard getting started, especially if you feel under pressure to be funny. So keep in mind that jokiness is not an essential feature of a cartoon; it must have a grain of truth or satire, but doesn't have to produce a belly-laugh.

Learning from others

Stealing someone else's ideas is obviously bad practice professionally, but it is not a bad way to learn your craft. If you see some cartoons where you like the joke or comment, but you think they aren't well drawn, try reworking them yourself. You can also do this with a cartoon that you particularly admire. The process of thinking it over and deciding how you could present it differently develops a useful habit of analysis.

Copying from the media in any form – animated cartoons as well as static ones – puts you in the area of copyright, which it is easy to breach, so use copying only as a form of private practice and don't even risk adapting an existing idea for publication.

Looking and listening

For original work, however, your sources are your every-day experience, including what you see and hear in the broadcasting media. You might have been in a funny or interesting situation that seems worth a comment, or been told about one by somebody else. If someone tells you a good joke, you might think of turning it into a strip of two or three images. You need to write it down and pare it down, because you don't want a lot of writing on the cartoon itself. Some very famous cartoonists can draw brilliantly but have no sense of a storyline, so you can also try working with a "words-person" who helps you to develop the sequence.

A joke delivers a punchline, and for a single cartoon it is usually the moment of delivery that is visualized. Focus strictly on the main event, and eliminate any distracting lead-in or surrounding detail. Rambling jokes can be very funny in conversation, but take too long on the page.

Surrealism is a type of humor that depends on non sequiturs or unexpected juxta-positions. Usually a person either has an inclination to this kind of humor or does not; it is hard to develop it objectively.

FURTHER INFORMATION

Observation, pages 96–97

From idea to finished art

On these pages, two artists have developed cartoons from the same given theme of the Empire State Building. Mooncat, top, and Rachael Ball, bottom, take the theme from initial rough notes and pencil sketches to final full-color image.

The building's appearance in *King Kong* is an early source of ideas

The twin towers of the World Trade Center muscle in on the Empire State's act

After rejecting King Kong, the club, the runaway, and the World Trade mafiosi, one idea, left, is chosen: the deflating building.

Like Mooncat, Rachael Ball begins with a sketch of the building. However, characters dominate her cartoons. Increasingly, figures are introduced and the building diminished until only a part of it is visible in the finished drawing.

The figure of a rejected character is doodled over the spire

▼ ► The wobbly image is made by photocopying a moving photograph. This is cut out and pasted up, right, with a copy of a stable city foreground and a drawn cartoon nipple valve, far right.

The gag reads more clearly with the valve on the right

FSSSSS.

FSSSSS.

mooncat

▲ ► The paste-up, above, is copied onto a thicker paper and the image finished, right, with watercolor washes to give the appearance of an inflatable Empire State Building.

► In this cartoon, it's not the choice of idea which gives the image its final form, but the choice of characters. The Empire State Building is both a symbol and the setting for a sidelong take on American society.

chew chew

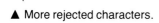
▲ More rejected characters.

► Sketches for the final image.

It was at the top of the Empire State Building that 6 year old Andrew pledged that one day America would know his true identity...
..That he, Andrew Newky was the long lost--King of America....!

..Not 2 yards away stood Jane Burke, Future President of the United-Communist States of America- Jane was a fierce Anti-Royalist And firm believer in capital punishment.

Pocket cartoons and political or topical features in newspapers and magazines often consist of a drawing with a typeset caption, but hand-lettering is still an important feature of single cartoons and strips. This must be clear and legible – fancy lettering styles are all very well, but readers will only try so hard for so long. Consistency is also a vital feature; any variation in size and proportion of lettering should have a logical reason, such as emphasis or display.

If you are no good at lettering, don't be tempted to make do. For commissioned work, tell your client that the lettering should be done by somebody else, or figure out another way of applying it, such as pasting in high-quality word processing (don't use typewriter script, which looks tacky). Poor lettering is a distraction and cannot be compensated by the most brilliant drawing, because it competes too strongly with the drawn message. Lettering naturally attracts the reader's attention.

Practice hand-lettering very assiduously. Fill pages and pages with letters, words, and sentences, paying careful attention to proportions and spacing (of individual letters, words, and lines). Keep working at it until you come to a point where you have achieved speed and accuracy, and the lettering remains consistent whatever you do.

There are various conventions for presenting written material within the cartoon. Speech balloons are usually ovals, rectangles with rounded corners, or irregular shapes billowing horizontally around the words. Thought balloons are like clouds, with undulating outlines. Loud or unexpected exclamations are sometimes put into balloons with zigzagging outlines. Captions that comment on the action – that is, are not directly spoken by the character in the frame – can be put into rectangular boxes at top or bottom of the cartoon.

Always write out the lettering before you draw the balloon; don't start by defining the boundary and then writing into the shape. Make sure that pointers from speech and thought balloons go straight to the right cartoon character. If more than one person is speaking within a single frame, make it clear in what order the words should be read. Balloons have a sort of artificial gravity; the first word balloon should be highest in the drawing and farthest to the left, the last is the lowest and farthest to the right. In languages that read left to right, that is a given rule that you shouldn't try to break.

For emphasis and sound effects, you can use fancy letters in black and white, or color if you are allowed it. There are all kinds of possible variations, including outlined letters, exploding letters, or heavily shadowed letterforms.

Lettering that needs to stand out can work very effectively in white on black. When you use color, make the colors of sound effects as clean, bright, and different from their surroundings as possible.

FURTHER INFORMATION

Devices, pages 58–59
Strips, pages 112–121

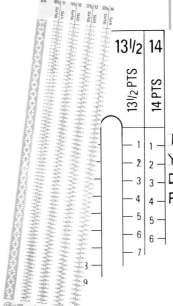

Line spacing
◄ Typesetting has instruments, such as the depth scales which measure lines of type and the spaces between them.

IF YOU WANT TO DO YOUR OWN LETTERING, DRAW PENCIL LINES FOR SPACING

▼ In standard comic lettering, the nearest equivalent to the depth scale is the Ames guide, which helps you draw evenly spaced parallel guidelines for as much lettering as you are likely to need in one balloon.

Letterspacing

UN EVEN

TOO WIDE

TOO TIGHT

CORRECT

▲ Like the drawing of characters themselves, the spaces between letters make your words. Getting this right needs practice. If the spaces between letters are irregular, open or too tight, the result may be that your letters strain legibility or do not form words.

Balloons

▲ Lettering containing dialogue and thought is usually separated from a cartoon's picture area by enclosure in a white graphic space with a linear border: the word balloon. The speech balloon's tail points from the center of the balloon to the mouth of the speaker.

Basic balloon shapes

▶ Clockwise from the top: thought, speech, exclamation, and caption. Try adapting them to convey expression.

I'LL NEVER DO WHAT YOU WANT ME TO-- NOT IN A MILLION YEARS...

I'LL NEVER DO WHAT YOU WANT ME TO-- NOT IN A MILLION YEARS!

I'LL NEVER DO WHAT YOU WANT ME TO-- NOT IN A MILLION YEARS!

Emphasis

There are two types of verbal emphasis in comic strips. One is contained inside balloons or captions and emulates the delivery of speech. The other is the sound effect, floating in the picture area and visually rendering auditory effects or human utterances.

AND THEY'LL ALL GET SOME! WILL YOU JUST RELAX?

▲ In word balloon emphasis, bold italic letters are a way of both fine-tuning the meaning and of producing graphic variety.

Sound-effect lettering

Sound-effect lettering does not have to obey the strict graphic rules that govern words inside balloons and captions. Use any type that suits your cartoon.

▲ Sound-effect lettering: the graphic equivalent of an explosion.

AAAAGHH!!

▲ More effect lettering, this time used for a human cry.

LIGHT & SHADE

You can use a variety of techniques for applying shading to your drawing, and the method you choose may depend on whether the cartoon is for reproduction and what are the limits of the reproduction process. That should be made clear to you in the brief you are given for the work. With regard to the visual qualities of shading, and what it adds to your image, you need to think very carefully about what function it serves, or whether you need it at all.

Shading relates to the three-dimensionality of objects and spaces and also to the mood and atmosphere of an image. You might use it for modeling – giving form and solidity to a figure, say – or for developing the drama of your setting. Visually, shading can be any degree of tone from very fine, light grays to dense, continuous black.

Experiment with lighting
Investigate the effectiveness of shading by making some drawings of real objects or scenes with a definite light source (experiment with different media too). Look for the ways the light and shadow explain the shapes of things, and pay attention to cast shadows, which provide the relationships of objects to the spaces they occupy, and can contribute a dramatic, almost abstract element. Then make the drawings again from memory, so that you have to consider the logic of the shading in relation to the light source. This way you develop a notional sense of how it works that you can apply to imaginary situations.

You can break the rules more easily once you know what they are. For example, you may draw a cartoon in which someone is strongly lit from above, but you don't choose to show the cast shadow on the ground. This might be just in order to simplify the drawing, or it might have a narrative function, to make the subject surreal or sinister.

FURTHER INFORMATION

Hatching, pages 80–81
Stippling, pages 110–111

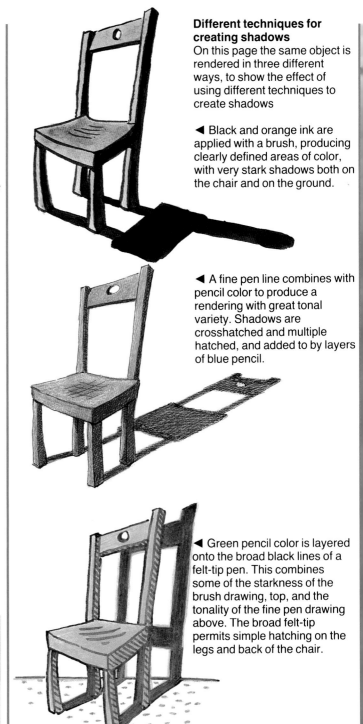

Different techniques for creating shadows
On this page the same object is rendered in three different ways, to show the effect of using different techniques to create shadows

◀ Black and orange ink are applied with a brush, producing clearly defined areas of color, with very stark shadows both on the chair and on the ground.

◀ A fine pen line combines with pencil color to produce a rendering with great tonal variety. Shadows are crosshatched and multiple hatched, and added to by layers of blue pencil.

◀ Green pencil color is layered onto the broad black lines of a felt-tip pen. This combines some of the starkness of the brush drawing, top, and the tonality of the fine pen drawing above. The broad felt-tip permits simple hatching on the legs and back of the chair.

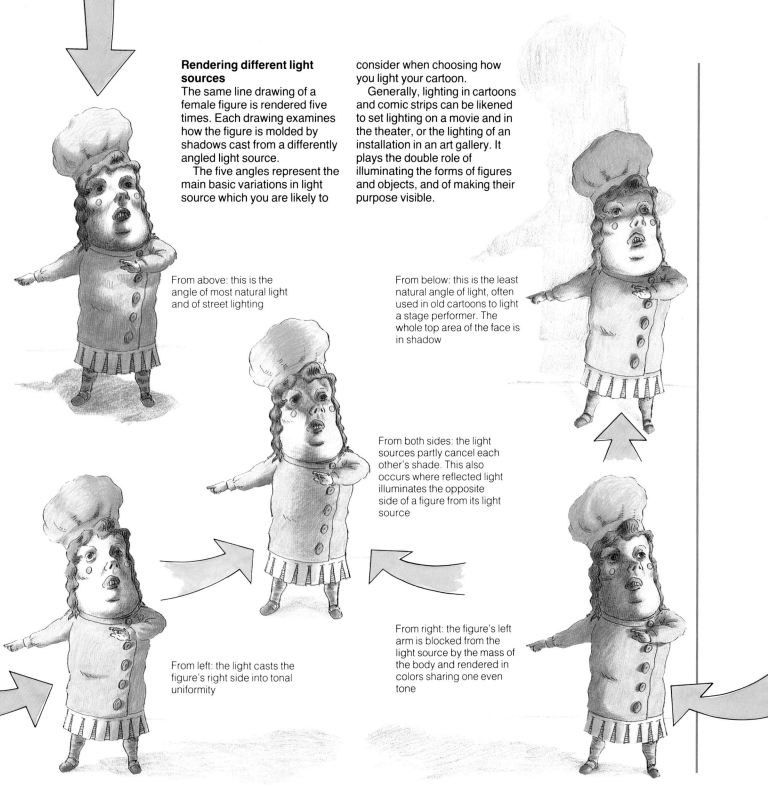

Rendering different light sources

The same line drawing of a female figure is rendered five times. Each drawing examines how the figure is molded by shadows cast from a differently angled light source.

The five angles represent the main basic variations in light source which you are likely to consider when choosing how you light your cartoon.

Generally, lighting in cartoons and comic strips can be likened to set lighting on a movie and in the theater, or the lighting of an installation in an art gallery. It plays the double role of illuminating the forms of figures and objects, and of making their purpose visible.

From above: this is the angle of most natural light and of street lighting

From below: this is the least natural angle of light, often used in old cartoons to light a stage performer. The whole top area of the face is in shadow

From both sides: the light sources partly cancel each other's shade. This also occurs where reflected light illuminates the opposite side of a figure from its light source

From left: the light casts the figure's right side into tonal uniformity

From right: the figure's left arm is blocked from the light source by the mass of the body and rendered in colors sharing one even tone

This method of shading cartoon drawings combines elegant, clear line with simple gray tone. It is a highly sensitive and accurate form of shading in black and white, suitable for subtle or delicate subjects and for creating atmosphere or texture. Technically, you apply the line work and allow it to dry, then brush in the gray on selected areas of the drawing, using heavily diluted ink; so the line work needs to be waterproof. A wash spreads more evenly if the area is already wetted with clean water – ideally, use separate brushes for water and tonal wash, to keep it absolutely clean.

As with spot color, you can alternatively apply the tone in non-repro blue, and the printer can prepare the plate mechanically so that the blue marks print gray. This method is used mainly in editorial and political cartoons and provides a different effect, but its roots are in the tradition of line and wash drawing.

Be cautious and economical when applying grays direct. Use one ready-mixed pale or mid-value gray; dark grays may become darker or fill in as solid black when reproduced. This is especially likely when the original is being reduced in size for print, which is usually the case. As you become more practiced in the technique and its effects, you may be able to develop a more variable painting method.

You can use washed tone simply to avoid leaving a line drawing too fragile and open; to shade or model space and form; or to create loose, fluid textures such as clouds, reflections, and half-shadows, where a heavy, holding black outline is inappropriate.

FURTHER INFORMATION

Color, pages 50–55
Light & Shade, pages 86–87

Simple wash
The more simple your line drawing, the more simple your washes are likely to be as a result.

▲ One simple, mid-toned wash is all that's needed to set this dinosaur cartoon against its blank white background. The slightly loose application keeps the image lively.

Variable wash
This sequence shows how different gradations of a wash are built up from light to dark, letting tones bleed softly into each other rather than creating hard-edged shapes. The artist has vignetted the wash around the light source, grading outward from the street light's central pool of brightness. This throws the background into deeper shadow and the figure into sharper relief.

1 The line drawing must be in waterproof ink and completely dry before you start work. Wet the paper with clean water and introduce a pale gray wash.

2 Use smaller areas of wash to strengthen the shapes. When adding cast shadows, make them much deeper in tone.

3 Be sparing with tonal detail in the figure directly under the light. It only needs a suggestion of shadow to show how the form curves away from the light source.

4 The gradual, wet-into-wet build-up of wash technique permits an extremely fine control of tone and texture.

Laying mechanical tints

An alternative to applying tone in a wash is to "lay" one or more mechanical tints. This has distinct advantages, chief among which is that the mechanical method retains the sharpness and clarity of your line drawing. In wash, the tonal variety of your drawing is reproduced by photographing the whole drawing – including the lines – as halftone dots.

By contrast, a tint is a flat area of dot tone. It's "mechanical" because it's included separately from your hand-drawn artwork. Tints come in varying densities, usually measured in increments of ten percent. Right, the same drawing is shown with a variety of tints.

▲ Two light tints are used on clothing, making sweatshirts the focus of this image. The tints also distinguish depths of picture with the darker, 20% tints on the foreground shirts and the lighter, 10%, tint on the mid-ground shirt.

▲ More tints are added to enhance the image, giving emphasis to the pants (50% black) and the scattered jumpers in the background (30% black).

▲ This final image makes the boldest statement of all: the hair is solid black and the number 13 on the shirt is picked out in 80% black.

Washes in context

▶ Light, mid-toned, and dark washes model form, light, and shadow in this cartoon. Pools of tone are shaped to leave highlights in almost every part of the picture.

In the right foreground is an exception to the wet-on-wet rule in wash. Here, pattern is superimposed on tone.

The floral decoration on the armchair is produced by letting the first, base wash dry and then working on top of it in mid-toned and dark washes to produce an impression of a rose-design chair covering.

"He got up one morning 8 years ago and said he was going to take a mulligan in the Game of Life, and I haven't seen him since."

Painting or drawing in any kind of medium is dependent on line – everything has a direction to it, and you are constantly dealing with the boundaries of shapes, even if they are not shown as strictly linear. In cartoons, of course, line is often the sole means of carrying the entire image, and the physical line qualities are crucial to the description and stylistic impact.

Line qualities depend on a number of factors: the actual implement or medium that you use to draw, the pressure on the paper, the potential for varying the weight and thickness of the line, and the continuity of the line. Consistency is important, but this doesn't mean that your lines are all of equal weight and value. A style of very nervous, scratchy, and broken lines is as effective as bold, even lines, provided you understand the range or limitations of your drawing method and apply it appropriately to your subject.

Line quality also relates to emphasis and focus within a cartoon. In a cartoon with lots of variable detail, evenly weighted lines throughout can cause different elements to compete too strongly. A background with perfect outlines can look less real than one with unfinished shapes.

When you buy a new drawing tool, fill several pages with random marks, just getting to know the feel of the instrument and the flow of the medium. Try everything, do everything – it is all drawing and it all works, there are no strictly right or wrong ways. You can even make good use of materials in less than perfect condition – a dried-up marker, for example, gives a pleasing soft, smudgy line. A dry mark is a slow mark, because the eye doesn't see it as a slick texture. Alternatively, if you make a drawing in clean, fine, flowing lines, then blacken them heavily, the whole image can change. There is a lot of room for experiment with this single element of cartoon drawing.

FURTHER INFORMATION

Brush Drawing, pages 40–41
Hatching, pages 80–81

Tools for different line qualities
Different tools can be used to create different effects.

The bullet-point marker gives a thick, strong and fluid line

A soft pencil can be used for both line and tone

Oil pastels leave a heavy, greasy texture

The brush is a versatile drawing tool, yielding fluent and varied lines

A fine, fiber-tipped marker is easy to use for cross-hatching and stipple

Conté crayon produces a line similar to a very soft pencil and areas of tone resembling pastel

Varieties of line
▲ Line is fine and even, done with fiber-tip or dip pen. Solid blacks add weight and depth.

▲ Brush drawing makes a fluid, swelling line that can help create shadowing, as on the man's forward leg.

▲ The nervous, scratchy line of a fine dip pen enhances a speedy sense of action, though the static background is less solid.

▲ An edged italic nib creates thick/thin variation when used for quick line work, seen here in the clothing and shadows.

In cartoon drawing, you can both depict movement directly and use devices that imply motion. The direct forms consist of shaping the subject obviously in action – through a particular configuration of limbs and body, a running man or a bounding dog is read as moving, even in isolation. More subtly, the angle and direction of the figure within the composition helps to emphasize the movement, perhaps from side to side of the picture or diagonally through the surroundings. If the person is coming straight toward you or going away, you can use exaggerated foreshortening to give direction.

Forms of implied movement commonly used to animate figures include multiple images, like time-lapse photographic frames. Related to this is the idea of blurring the image of the moving part, whether it is single or multiple, suggesting an out-of-focus photo. There are also simplified devices – whizzy speed lines trailing from behind a moving person or vehicle; the arc of parallel lines that traces, for example, the motion of a hand and arm coming down in a mighty blow. These distinctly non-real devices are common currency in cartoons. Juxtaposition is a simple but relatively sophisticated solution. You cannot define speed and direction if everything is moving, but if you provide a recognizably slow or fixed reference point, some movement is obvious by comparison. This can be real, symbolic, and associative, as in the image of the hare and tortoise race, or located firmly in the everyday world, as with a person running to catch a bus that has halted.

FURTHER INFORMATION

Clothing, pages 46–49
Figures, pages 68–71

Schematic drawings
These drawings have been made from a wooden lay figure with movable parts, a useful though not essential aid in studying the way the body works in movement.

The momentum of the outstretched arm is pulling the whole body in the same direction

Arms spread to anticipate and balance forward momentum

Lunging creates dramatic foreshortening of the legs

A rhythmic movement like this could be dance

Widespread legs balance dramatic upper body movement

A knockout blow splays limbs and pushes back head

▼ A cycle of movement can be seen as individual poses that become more and more exaggerated. The cartoon figure can go even further, producing an action that is not possible in the real world. To show suggested movement with only one image, consider which part of the cycle will provide the most descriptive, dramatic, or funny pose in the given context.

Types of movement
The schematic figures show different kinds of movement. Whatever the style in which you may choose to draw, such figures provide the basic building blocks for you to use.

▶ This foreshortened view with arms fully extended has a kind of freefall momentum which could be moving up or down.

▼ When this pose is turned into a basketball player, it is obvious that the movement is a leap, not a fall.

▼ The body counters movement of a left limb by opposite movement of a right, and vice versa. In a running pose, arms and legs move rhythmically in opposite directions.

▼ The cartoon character's fluid, simple shapes obey the same rules of opposite stresses.

MOVEMENT
SWIPEFILE

This swipefile contains a range of images by different cartoonists for you to copy or adapt. Use it to help you to explore ideas about style, technique, and characterization.

▲ With only one hand on the ground, the figure is about to topple.

▲ Angle of body indicates this is again unlikely to be the perfect handstand.

◀ The energetic ballet movement of this female clown is a stylized image of the body in flight.

Oil pastel and pen speed lines emphasize direction of motion

Cartoon exaggeration shows the body out of contact with the ground

zigzag outline suggests shock waves running through body

▶ The tilt of the body is so extreme that balance cannot be regained.

The shadow places the body in space. Hold a finger over the shadow and the figure appears to be in free fall, and could be at any height

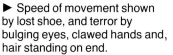

▶ Speed of movement shown by lost shoe, and terror by bulging eyes, clawed hands and, hair standing on end.

94

► Bent legs and forward thrust of torso mark the figure as a skater.

Movement reinforced by flow of hair and speed lines

Matching the color of speed lines to a figure's hair personalizes the image and accentuates the danger

The player's hair indicates the direction of his motion

Solid colors emphasize the immobility of a body in free fall

▲ The effect of gravity is indicated by the presence of speed lines and by the distance between falling figure and ground.

► In this line drawing of a runner, color has been added rapidly, accentuating the implied movement.

Exaggerating the angle of the body from the vertical emphasizes motion

▼ Horizontal lines of horse's body, flowing mane, unseated rider and speed lines combine in an expressive image.

▲ Movement in this image centers on the position of the ball. The player has angled his body in readiness for a kick.

Grass provides the static element to contrast with the violence of movement

A cartoonist's job is to observe and comment. Style and technique can be developed just through practicing your drawing, but the raw material of your cartoons comes from the real world. Keeping a sketchbook enables you to gather vast amounts of information and inspiration which you can draw upon for whole images or incidental details in your work. Start to develop a habit of scribbling things down as you see them – a sketchbook is like a visual diary of your day-to-day experience.

Since the point of this exercise is information-gathering, don't try to take your sketchbook notes in cartoon form, or you will find that you have eliminated useful material too early. Note down what you see as accurately and expressively as you can in the time; an eye for the important feature, and the technical ability to capture it, improves with practice. Look out for the characterful people, descriptive poses and gestures, typical or unusual settings, and useful props. If you are pushed for time, you don't have to draw everything; take written notes as well to remind yourself of how people behaved or how the situation developed, and atmospheric background such as colors and lighting.

On a practical level, keep it simple. Your sketchbook should travel with you everywhere, ready for use at a moment's notice. Buy a small, sturdy sketchbook, hardback or ring-bound, containing good-quality drawing paper. Make sure you are equipped with a pencil, fiber-tip pen, or ballpoint at all times.

Sketching from life
Drawing from observation is a way of helping you remain fresh and less prone to graphic clichés. The sketchbook drawings assembled here show how regular practice is not oriented to the production of finished images but to the drawing process itself. They also indicate the importance of seeking out likely places to find your subjects.

This pencil sketch of a row of houses includes interesting attention to brickwork

Precision and detail are the keynotes of this pencil drawing of a store front

This seaside scene contains an unusual view of small boats and yachts

A soft graphite pencil is the most adaptable of tools, suitable for quick, fluid figure drawings

No scene is built from these tidy studies of figures and faces

Exploring ideas
Knowing the overall impression
he wants to create – of a pub
with lighted frontage standing
against a darkening sky – the
artist sketches outdoors to
explore different versions of the
basic idea, eventually coming
on one that conveys exactly the
right image.

▶ This is a simple visualization
sketch, before any research is
done to find the location.

DUSK
SKY

lamp-
post?

Pool of light

▶ A building with a
taller but more
compact, stronger
shape seems a
better choice, and
offers a lot of
interesting
incidental detail.

tiles   little hanging
            baskets

BASIC IDEA

▶ An actual example roughly
sketched on location supplies
the basic shape of the
drawing.

SIGN

DOG &
DUCK

▲ The picturesque
character of this
building made it a
strong candidate
for the final
choice.

RISING TROUT

▲ The cartoon had to be black-
and-white only, so the artist
chose to use ink line with solid
blacks and two types of

mechanical tints to deal with the
shadowy night effect. The
clouds are treated with crayon.

The classic system for creating an illusion of three-dimensional space and form on a two-dimensional surface, perspective can be used in a simple or complex way in cartooning, but invariably increases the impact of the drawing. To a certain extent, the effects of perspective can be judged by eye, but giving yourself a basic grid to work to makes the rendering easier and more consistent.

If your cartoon characters are not shown in any context – as isolated figures or a head-to-head arrangement – then you don't have to worry about perspective. But as soon as you have an implied background space or situation, the viewer will subconsciously expect it to conform to basic rules of perspective, because we have been taught to read spatial information in this way. Total distortion or "non-real" space needs to have justification in the cartoon idea.

Vanishing points
Perspective is based on a horizon line, which may be observed or notional, and one or more vanishing points fixed on the horizon. In one-point perspective, all horizontal lines receding from the viewer go to one vanishing point. Verticals are fixed, and horizontals parallel to the horizon remain horizontal. This is the equivalent of looking straight down the street; the roadsides appear to converge on the horizon, and houses lining the street appear smaller with increasing distance. In two-point perspective, you have two vanishing points at some distance from each other on the horizon; receding horizontals go to one or other point. This is illustrated by the idea of standing at a street corner able to see down two streets at once.

Three-point perspective enables you to emphasize distance upward or downward. It works similarly to two-point perspective, but verticals also converge on a vanishing point. If they converge upward, you have what is known as the worm's-eye view; imagine being at ground level in front of a corner building, able to see down two streets and up the front of the building simultaneously (this is not a normal kind of vision, as in such a situation you tend to focus on things sequentially rather than all at once). In the aerial or bird's-eye view, the third vanishing point is below the building, so the walls appear to converge downward.

There are practical problems of using perspective when your drawing is relatively small-scale. The vanishing points in two- and three-point perspective are typically off the paper for an exterior view, for example; if you bring them in more closely the distortion is immense. A building never recedes to a single point – it always has to have a base, or it looks unreal. However, you can use the principle broadly as a guideline, without setting up complicated arrangements to locate vanishing points halfway across your studio.

Once you have set up a perspective for an interior or exterior view, all objects and figures are governed by the arrangement. People on the street, for example, appear smaller as they get farther away; their heads and feet touch converging lines of recession at any given level. Inside a room, the walls and ceiling recede in perspective, so does a table in the middle of the room, so does a box on the table.

One-point perspective is far the easiest method to use, and in terms of cartoon shorthand, it does an effective job. But if you are looking for more sophisticated and/or realistic effects, you may need to grapple with two- or three-point perspective. The examples given here show you the basics of each order and its applications; if you are specially interested in systems of this kind, you can easily find further information in specialized perspective manuals.

FURTHER INFORMATION

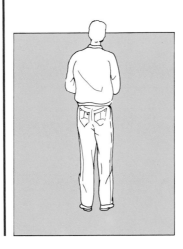

The horizon line
▼ Perspective alters as soon as you move your viewpoint, because the horizon line, which dictates the vanishing point or points, is your own eye level. If you are drawing from memory or imagination, invent your viewpoint and make it consistent.

One-point perspective

▶ Draw a horizon line – representing your eye level – and fix a vanishing point on it. The farther the point is to one side, the more objects on that side are compressed. Vertical planes that face you are drawn flat-on and undistorted. Lines can then be drawn back from corners and edges to the vanishing point to create the sides of a cubic shape that recedes directly away from you. In a solid shape you see the underside if the object is above the horizon line, the top plane if the object is below. But you can also treat them as hollow forms. Make construction lines in pencil, then ink the appropriate shapes.

▶ In this street scene, the notional viewpoint is directly in the center, hence the central vanishing point. If the artist were to move to the right, it would be left of center.

▶ Simple one-point perspective does its job well here, explaining the spatial context of the characters without presenting complex drawing problems. Note the cartoonist has not slavishly followed the rules of one-point perspective but the drawing works nonetheless.

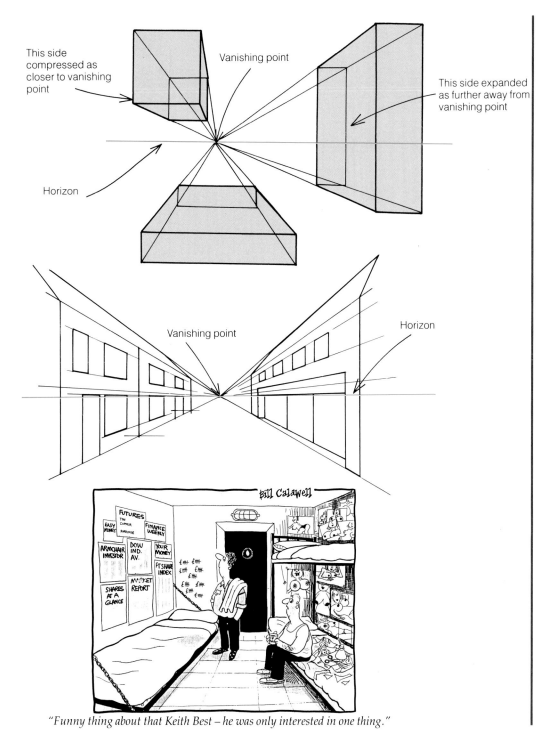

This side compressed as closer to vanishing point

Vanishing point

This side expanded as further away from vanishing point

Horizon

Vanishing point

Horizon

Bill Caldwell

"Funny thing about that Keith Best – he was only interested in one thing."

Two-point perspective

▶ In two-point perspective, site vanishing points at either side of the horizon line. You then begin a cubic shape with the closest vertical edge, from which both sides recede. Relation to the horizon line still fixes viewpoint from above, below, or level.

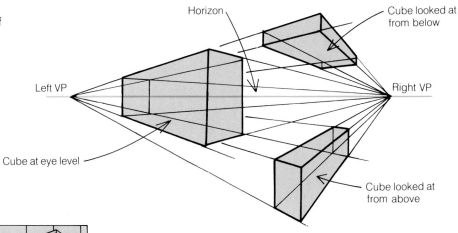

Horizon

Cube looked at from below

Left VP

Right VP

Cube at eye level

Cube looked at from above

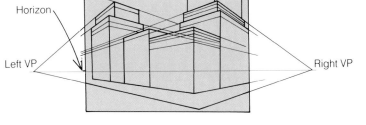

Horizon

Left VP

Right VP

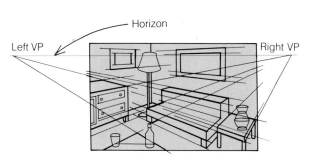

Horizon

Left VP

Right VP

▲ In an interior, you would get a distorted view if both vanishing points were on the paper. But you can make a grid suggesting line covergence outside the frame, on which you can plot flat surfaces in perspective, such as tabletops and pictures on a wall.

◀ A classic example of two-point perspective. The left-hand edge of the steps lead off to the left-hand vanishing point, and the side of the podium gives off to the right.

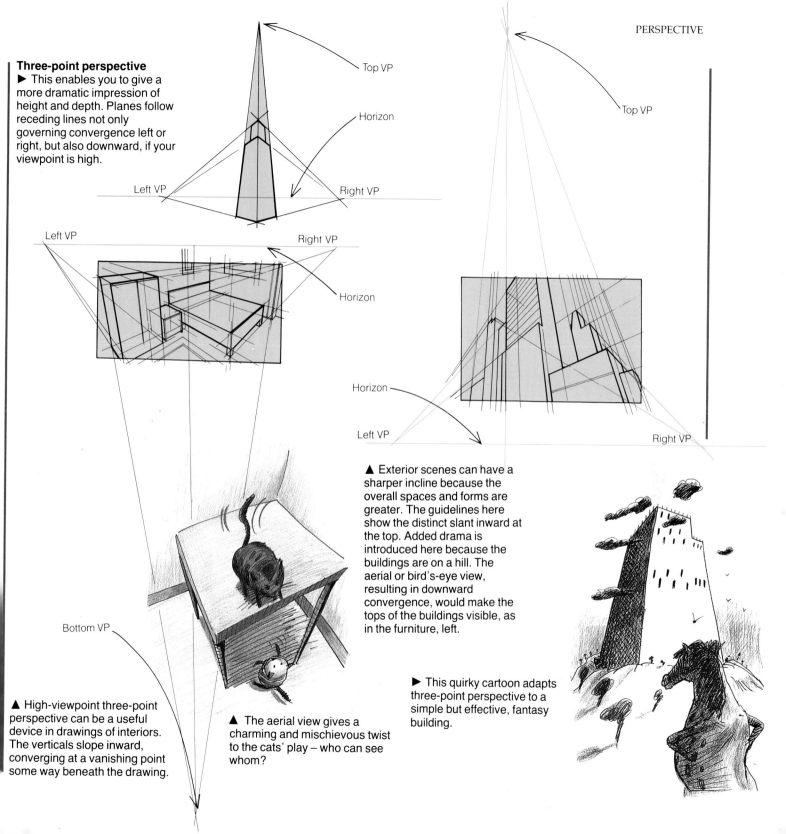

Top VP

Horizon

Three-point perspective
► This enables you to give a more dramatic impression of height and depth. Planes follow receding lines not only governing convergence left or right, but also downward, if your viewpoint is high.

Top VP

Left VP   Right VP

Left VP   Right VP

Horizon

Horizon

Horizon

Left VP   Right VP

Bottom VP

▲ High-viewpoint three-point perspective can be a useful device in drawings of interiors. The verticals slope inward, converging at a vanishing point some way beneath the drawing.

▲ The aerial view gives a charming and mischievous twist to the cats' play – who can see whom?

▲ Exterior scenes can have a sharper incline because the overall spaces and forms are greater. The guidelines here show the distinct slant inward at the top. Added drama is introduced here because the buildings are on a hill. The aerial or bird's-eye view, resulting in downward convergence, would make the tops of the buildings visible, as in the furniture, left.

► This quirky cartoon adapts three-point perspective to a simple but effective, fantasy building.

PRESENTATION & PUBLICATION

There are some obvious publishing categories that seem ideal targets for presentation of your work, but any area of illustration work is highly competitive and you need to think about the opportunities as broadly as possible.

Newspapers and magazines

For these publications, as well as specified cartoon pages or columns, material may be needed for fillers, say, if a story falls short. Take a look at what kind of cartoons different publications include, the drawing styles (line, tone, or color), and the average number of cartoons reproduced in an issue.

Reference libraries provide you with two sources of research: one, a range of newspapers and magazines kept in general stock for local readers, including current and back numbers; two, reference manuals for artists and writers listing the addresses of publishers and publications nationwide. Beware of just picking out a magazine title and sending material on chance. It is easy for an editor or art director to spot that you haven't the first idea of what their publication is like; try to find out what they want.

When you think of magazines, you may get an image of commercial glossies, joke and puzzle mags, or journals with serious political and social comment. But keep an eye out for smaller operations such as fanzines and in-house newsletters that might be good starting points. Ask around your friends and local contacts for further ideas.

- Local newspapers
- National newspapers
- Weekly national magazines
- Monthly national magazines
- Special-interest magazines
- Trade papers and magazines
- Local listings magazines
- Fanzines
- In-house newsletters of local businesses and institutions

Cartoon illustration

Books of cartoon collections are mainly restricted to famous names, and it is unusual for general books to be fully illustrated in cartoon style, unless by a big name to help publicity. But it is not unheard of, and you can research the possibilities in this area. There are also some opportunities in advertising, design, and merchandising. You can start by aiming for direct involvement with local businesses which might need, say, a logotype or a drawing for a promotional flier, or look up art agencies and design groups listed in contact directories.

- Adult non-fiction publishers
- Children's book publishers
- Comic book publishers
- Artists' agents
- Advertising agencies
- Design groups
- Illustration studios

Syndication agencies

These are agencies whose business it is to distribute certain types of published material to various media outlets within a defined geographical area, nationwide or worldwide. A number are dedicated to hard news stories and pictures, others handle the lighter side of publishing, including items such as feature articles, horoscopes, and cartoons. Generally, you will need to be professionally well established before your work has syndication potential and it is inadvisable to send unsolicited original material.

Record-keeping

All graphic artists and illustrators will advise you that at first you can expect to paper a wall with rejection slips. The only solution is to persevere. There is nothing to prevent you from reapplying to a publisher after a lapse of time – people's requirements and tastes change, and your work will also have progressed.

Targeting different publications
▼ The overall layout and style of newspapers and magazines often naturally makes room for one-off humorous cartoons and topical cartoons. General non-fiction books also sometimes use cartoons.

General non-fiction books sometimes feature cartoons as fillers or to convey editorial information

However, sending the same work back to someone who has recently rejected it, addressing it to an outdated contact, or mixing up the covering letters when you are sending several batches are all signs of a lack of professionalism. It is worth keeping careful records of what you have sent out and what was the response, along the following lines:

- The name of your contact and the company he or she works for.
- List of work supplied. Photocopy the cartoons for your own reference and give them titles or numbers that you can easily record. It is important you know what you have shown to whom, and whether or not work has been published and should not be sent out again.
- Date work was sent out; response received; publication date if accepted; date when rejected work was returned.
- Payment agreed for publication. Keep invoices and accounts of income and expenses as separate records.

Presenting yourself

Presenting yourself effectively involves some initial expense, but when you are contacting busy professionals, it helps you to claim attention. A printed letterhead can be used as a compliments slip and for invoicing, as well as for letters. If you are prepared for some extra outlay, a business card is handier for the recipient to keep in a phone or card file than a letter sheet.

The least expensive way to produce a letterhead is to run it off yourself on a good-quality word processor. This will limit your choices for layout and typeface. If you want to include a logo or cartoon with typeset name, address, phone, fax, etc, you can do a camera-ready layout for commercial printing. Get several printers' quotes, as costs vary widely.

A well-designed signature, logo, or small-scale cartoon gives a clear identity that sticks in people's minds. Once you have artwork, you can use and reuse it for any kind of personal stationery, or even for a display ad in a local or trade paper.

As you have cartoons published, you might like to produce a mail-out sheet showing several samples with your letterhead or logo. Good-quality photocopies may be adequate for this, but if you want a large quantity it may be cheaper to print. The cartoonist has an advantage over other illustrators in that

Recipient					
Fly fishing weekly – Dave Salmon, Art Editor.					
Cartoons sent	Date	Accepted	Rejected & returned	Payment	Publishing date
numbers 18, 19, 20, 22, 48	2nd Jan	18, 19	20, 22, 48	£60	March issue

Recipient				
Woodworkers monthly, Tim Pinewood, Cartoon Editor.				
Cartoons sent	Date	Accepted	Rejected & returned	
3, 6, 7, 19 + 20, 22	21st Jan	7, 20	3, 6, 19, 20 22	

Cataloging cartoons
▲ Keep a careful record of what you have sent out and whether or not you were successful in getting the cartoon into print. Include information such as whether the artwork has been returned, payment and publication date.

Going about it
To avoid wasting time, effort and expense, follow a few simple guidelines when making your contacts:

- Make sure you have an up-to-date address for the publication or agency you are applying to. Even the largest companies can move premises and reference listings sometimes republish outdated information. Telephone to check an address if the company is unfamiliar to you.
- Study the areas of special interest in the publication and the way their cartoons are presented, to make sure that both the style and content of your work will be appropriate.
- Sending to a named editor or art director is much more effective than enclosing a generalized cover note. When deciding who to target, keep in mind that the editorial content of your cartoons may be as important as the drawing style in catching someone's eye. For large-scale journals, check whether there is a specialist cartoon editor.

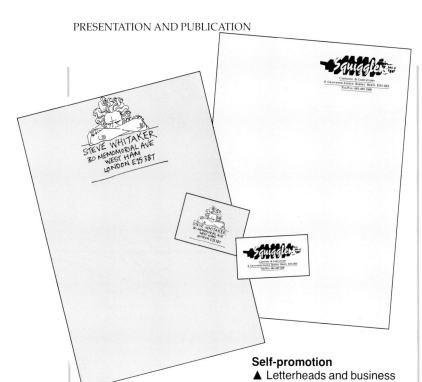

Self-promotion
▲ Letterheads and business cards should be functional and at the same time catch the art director's eye.

you can usually show off your work very well without any color, which greatly adds to print costs.

Pitching in person
In most circumstances, you do not need a personal appointment to make initial contacts. Where cartoons are basically throwaway items, as in newspapers, you may not meet the editor face to face even after you have started to supply work. If you are trying to enter the field of book or advertising illustration, however, presenting directly to an editor or art director provides a better opportunity for both of you to see what the other might have to offer.

The golden rules are to make an appointment in advance, by telephone or letter, arrive on time, and make sure your portfolio is organized. Do not unload a sea of paper scraps on someone's desk and hope they'll be struck by your talent and originality. Professional presentation is part of an illustrator's skill.

If you have printed samples from previous commissions, include these in your portfolio.

Pitching by mail
Whenever you send uncommissioned material to someone, you are adding another small task to their workload. You need to make a good impression quickly, so this means presenting your work directly and cleanly.

Take time to construct a brief, businesslike covering letter which you can use as a standard form for making new contacts. If you want rejected work returned, enclose a self-addressed, stamped envelope.

Be careful not to misrepresent your work by sending poor photocopies. Make sure that the illustrations are sharp and black, that the qualities of the drawing show up well, and that captions or speech bubbles have clean contrast and even tone.

You should expect that whoever receives your work will deal with it in a professional manner. However, it occasionally happens that by accident or design, submitted work gets into print without the artist being notified. A good-quality photocopy can be used as an original. If you are worried about this when sending off precious samples to an outfit whose reputation you do not know, you can photocopy on red paper, which registers similarly to black on a process camera, so preventing reproduction from the copy.

Organizing a portfolio
▼ Ideally use a small portoflio containing plastic sleeves which protect and display work. You can then arrange your cartoons in a suitable sequence, relate images to each other, and flip over pages easily to make points as you discuss work.

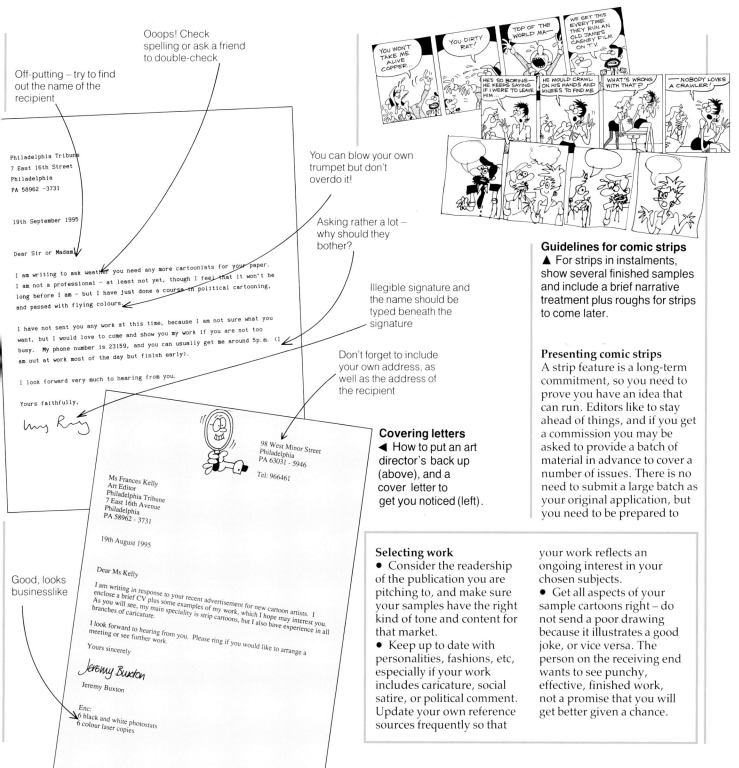

Off-putting – try to find out the name of the recipient

Ooops! Check spelling or ask a friend to double-check

You can blow your own trumpet but don't overdo it!

Asking rather a lot – why should they bother?

Illegible signature and the name should be typed beneath the signature

Don't forget to include your own address, as well as the address of the recipient

Good, looks businesslike

Philadelphia Tribune
7 East 16th Street
Philadelphia
PA 58962 -3731

19th September 1995

Dear Sir or Madam,

I am writing to ask weather you need any more cartoonists for your paper. I am not a professional – at least not yet, though I feel that it won't be long before I am – but I have just done a course in political cartooning, and passed with flying colours.

I have not sent you any work at this time, because I am not sure what you want, but I would love to come and show you my work if you are not too busy. My phone number is 23159, and you can usually get me around 5p.m. (I am out at work most of the day but finish early).

I look forward very much to hearing from you.

Yours faithfully,

Ms Frances Kelly
Art Editor
Philadelphia Tribune
7 East 16th Avenue
Philadelphia
PA 58962 - 3731

98 West Minor Street
Philadelphia
PA 63031 - 5946

Tel: 966461

19th August 1995

Dear Ms Kelly

I am writing in response to your recent advertisement for new cartoon artists. I enclose a brief CV plus some examples of my work, which I hope may interest you. As you will see, my main speciality is strip cartoons, but I also have experience in all branches of caricature.

I look forward to hearing from you. Please ring if you would like to arrange a meeting or see further work.

Yours sincerely

Jeremy Buxton

Jeremy Buxton

Enc:
6 black and white photostats
6 colour laser copies

Covering letters
◄ How to put an art director's back up (above), and a cover letter to get you noticed (left).

Guidelines for comic strips
▲ For strips in instalments, show several finished samples and include a brief narrative treatment plus roughs for strips to come later.

Presenting comic strips
A strip feature is a long-term commitment, so you need to prove you have an idea that can run. Editors like to stay ahead of things, and if you get a commission you may be asked to provide a batch of material in advance to cover a number of issues. There is no need to submit a large batch as your original application, but you need to be prepared to

Selecting work
• Consider the readership of the publication you are pitching to, and make sure your samples have the right kind of tone and content for that market.
• Keep up to date with personalities, fashions, etc, especially if your work includes caricature, social satire, or political comment. Update your own reference sources frequently so that your work reflects an ongoing interest in your chosen subjects.
• Get all aspects of your sample cartoons right – do not send a poor drawing because it illustrates a good joke, or vice versa. The person on the receiving end wants to see punchy, effective, finished work, not a promise that you will get better given a chance.

work up further ideas quickly and visualize future strips.

Present several finished samples to show that your drawing style is competent and consistent, that you can keep up the presentation of a character in different poses and contexts, and that your gag lines or narrative are also continuously high standard.

If your idea is a storytelling strip cut into installments, you need not draw the whole thing to reproduction quality. You can provide finished examples together with a brief narrative treatment of how the story continues. You might also include roughs for a couple of strips to come later in the sequence if these would have special visual impact or an interesting twist.

You've got a job!
If you have submitted cartoon copies and something is selected, all you have to do is send the original artwork. If your submissions inspire somone to commission work on a specific topic, make sure you find out all you need to know about the job before you start.

● Sizing artwork – check what the dimensions or proportions

From brief to printed piece
◄ You may be given a written or verbal brief. Make sure you understand exactly what is required before you begin work.

Sizing up artwork
Draw a diagonal from the bottom left corner through the top right and extend it beyond the rectangle.

of the printed piece will be, and whether the editor wants the original to be same-size or larger.

● Medium – is this a black-and-white piece or color? If black and white, is it for reproduction in line only (hard blacks and whites), or can half-tones (grays) be included? If it is color, is it full-color artwork or are separate overlays needed to indicate color tints?

● Base material – it is sometimes essential to present artwork on flexible support, so that it can be wrapped onto a drum when scanned for reproduction. If you prefer to use rigid artboard, check that

this is acceptable.

● Words – are captions and speech bubbles to be handwritten or typeset, laid out directly on the artwork or presented on overlay sheets?

● Fee – find out if there is a standard fee or, if asked to quote, try to figure out how long it will take you to complete the cartoon and what it is worth at an hourly rate.

● Roughs – you may be asked to present rough sketches showing more than one approach, or a pencil rough for approval before you start a finished version. Minor amendments, if requested, are part of the job, but if a client changes the original idea and wants you to rework the image substantially, try to renegotiate your terms.

● Deadlines – fix the dates for supplying roughs and/or finished artwork and meet your deadlines at all costs. If you feel a proposed deadline is certainly unrealistic, either negotiate an extension up-

ARTIST'S BRIEF: DOG FACTS

About the book 160-page , 4-colour book, instant reference manual for dog-lovers, packed with information. Mostly hard info but some "fact boxes" lightened by inclusion of cartoons interpreting the text.

Content of cartoons Quirky fact boxes appear every 3/4 spreads, and it is these which we want to illustrate with (equally quirky) cartoons. Please can you read relevant text box and interpret them freely. Remember readership can take some gentle fun being poked at pooches, and play up, too, the special relationship between man and dog.

Illustration style Pen (b&w). keep art simple. No backgrounds.

Number of cartoons required 40 a/ws in total.

Size Work twice up, following layout supplied.

Checking stages Supply pencil roughs for approval before going to final art. See separate sheet for schedule.

▲ You will usually be asked to supply pencil roughs for approval by the art director. Minor amendments may be requested at this stage.

▼ Revised pencil roughs, showing amendments and refinements. The next stage is to go to finished artwork.

front or refuse the work; do not use tight timing as an excuse for failing to deliver.

Supplying finished artwork

When you are sending original work to the client, make sure it is well protected, both by secure packaging and by the mail service that you choose. Special postage rates that insure contents and guarantee rapid delivery are expensive, but so is loss of your precious package.

Finished artwork is usually presented with a mask, or mat frame, bordering the image, and a protective cover paper or acetate sheet over the mask. If the artwork itself has a broad border, you can attach the mat frame with two-sided tape. Otherwise, position the cartoon on a backing board and attach the mat and cover sheet to the board.

To avoid flexible artwork being crushed in the mail, send it in a cardboard-backed envelope or slip a piece of cardboard into an ordinary envelope to make it rigid.

Your signature

You will have noticed that famous cartoonists usually make sure their signatures are prominently displayed. These are often designed as a kind of logo, as well as simply identifying the artist. Start by deciding who you want to be. You can use your full name, first name, or surname only, or an invented "pen-name" (in which case make sure your invoices also show the name that will enable you to bank the payment). Avoid anything too similar to someone already well known.

Contract terms

Many publishing agreements are surprisingly informal, but you should ask for a letter of agreement confirming the conditions of work, deadlines, and fee. If your client fails to

Straight dealings

• Once you have agreed a fee and deadline, it is up to you to keep to both. You have no right to more time or money just because the work takes longer than you estimated. If a real disaster may prevent you from delivering on time, let the client know as soon as you do, so he or she can cancel or reschedule.
• Stick to the brief. Even if you have a "better" idea halfway through a job, you

are commissioned to supply what the client has asked for.
• Always be polite and courteous, even if you are treated unfairly – it is never a good idea to burn your bridges.
• Do not criticize someone else's work or publication to an actual or potential client. It makes a bad impression if you talk yourself up at another person's expense, and your client or colleagues may assume you would do the same to them.

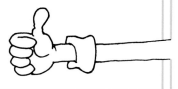

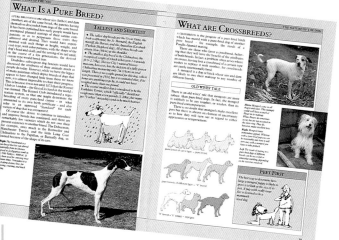

▲ Your cartoon in its printed form. Check to see if it's part of your contract that you get a copy of the finished book.

provide written confirmation, you can make your own job sheet outlining the brief and terms discussed, and send it in. This is a safeguard if, for any reason, the terms seem to change as the work progresses. However, it is worth remembering that most people have no intention of disadvantaging you – they want the work and will pay if you perform competently. Informality is fine if you feel confident of the situation.

Make sure you know the position with regard to ownership of the original artwork and its copyright. You have the right to return of the artwork unless you have signed something that says otherwise. Copyright will usually be with the publisher; for advertising and book illustration work, you may be asked to assign copyright

totally, so the image can be published in any market your client enters without further reference to you. Alternatively, you may be surrendering rights to specific uses only. Check contract terms carefully with regard to this issue, so that you know exactly what you have agreed to when you sign.

FURTHER INFORMATION

Strips, pages 112–121

Cartoons are full of stock characters, but the kind of stereotypes that might cause offense are rapidly disappearing. There are borderline areas where it can be difficult to tell whether something that makes you laugh could seem offensive to somebody else, but you need to avoid tired old assumptions about what particular groups or types of people are like.

Stereotyping is generalization, and there are certain conventions which we easily "read" and understand, though they bear no relation to reality. The prisoner in a suit covered with arrows, and the burglar's striped jersey and mask are shorthand of this kind – their origins are obscure, but the visual symbolism is picked up by new generations. However, librarians are now rarely dowdy people wearing pince-nez eyeglasses, and it is no longer particularly appropriate to show them as such; but big business is often represented by rather faceless men in suits, and that image works slightly differently and more acceptably.

Uniforms are useful stereotyping because they identify without personalizing. You need to think about the function of your drawing, why you want to generalize and what your rendering is saying. Remember that all generalization is potentially offensive to someone, and you have to decide where you draw the line.

Settings can also be stereotypical – the desert island with the single palm tree, identical skyscrapers in a modern city, or the rocks and bristling cacti that symbolize the Old West. Shorthand symbols are valuable because you have to set your scene very fast. But rather than depend on ancient clichés, you can develop a set of types in people, settings, or props that is based on your own observation of the world around you. Unfamiliar subjects can be gleaned from television, magazines, and other media sources.

FURTHER INFORMATION

Clothing, pages 46–49
Figures, pages 68–71

Costume and settings
Each of these stereotyped figures is pictured with props and in the kind of background setting which reinforces their stereotyping. They are inseparable from their settings and vice versa.

▲ The schoolteacher in cartoons is identified principally through costume and expression – archaic dress and an unbending manner.

▲ The garbage man is the stereotype of the happy working man, grimily toiling for the good of society. Hard physical labor has made his body big. His habitat is an idealized suburbia comprising row upon row of identical houses.

▲ The stereotype of the nurse is identified by her uniform and sex. Although not all nurses are female, this has become a stereotype that is readily understood. The uniform ties the figure visually into the institution of which she is a part, and the bed-ridden patient stresses her occupation.

▲ Burglary may not be an "official" profession, but a burglar is a professional in his way. Typically, he is a creature of the night, straying into the prosperous homes from which he would certainly be excluded in the daytime.

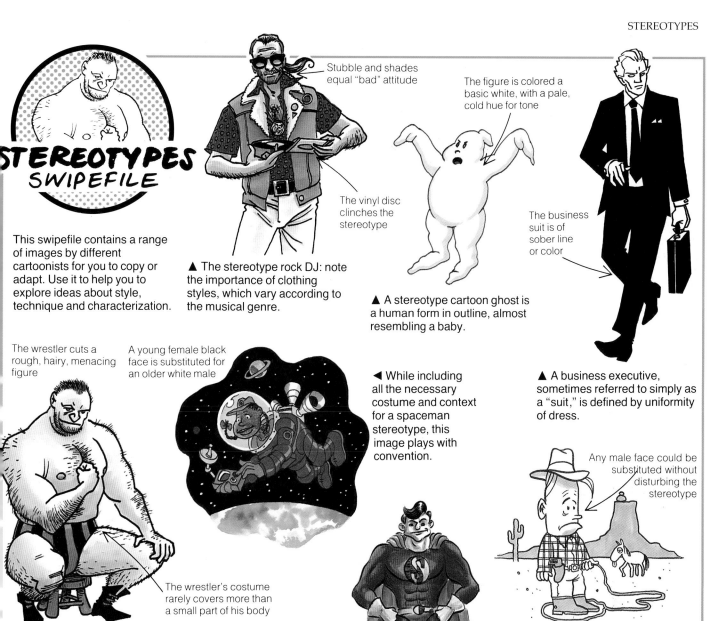

STEREOTYPES
SWIPEFILE

This swipefile contains a range of images by different cartoonists for you to copy or adapt. Use it to help you to explore ideas about style, technique and characterization.

Stubble and shades equal "bad" attitude

The vinyl disc clinches the stereotype

▲ The stereotype rock DJ: note the importance of clothing styles, which vary according to the musical genre.

The figure is colored a basic white, with a pale, cold hue for tone

▲ A stereotype cartoon ghost is a human form in outline, almost resembling a baby.

The business suit is of sober line or color

▲ A business executive, sometimes referred to simply as a "suit," is defined by uniformity of dress.

The wrestler cuts a rough, hairy, menacing figure

A young female black face is substituted for an older white male

◄ While including all the necessary costume and context for a spaceman stereotype, this image plays with convention.

Any male face could be substituted without disturbing the stereotype

The wrestler's costume rarely covers more than a small part of his body

▲ The figure of the wrestler, like the superhero, also stereotypes male bodily characteristics.

The exaggerated musculature is lightly rendered

▶ The superhero genre figure, satirized here, stereotypes mainly male bodily characteristics.

Generic costume and cape are juxtaposed with "girly" pink slippers

▲ The cowboy is identified by his Stetson, boots, and lasso, as well as by the background, with rocks and cactus.

Stippling is a form of non-directional shading, consisting of masses of small dots or similar marks. The marks don't have to be even or regularly sized and shaped – if you want that effect you are better off using mechanical tints.

Stippling can contain any kind of small-scale mark, such as tiny splotches, ticks, hooks, blobs, or even miniscule images. The effect you get depends partly on the materials you use.

Non-directional shading is both an advantage and a disadvantage in drawing. It is relatively quiet and unobtrusive; it doesn't drag your eye across the page, but it tends to be fairly static, even serene. Linear shading is more dynamic, but if you want a calming effect of variable tone, stippling is ideal. It is not suitable for speedy subjects, such as a train whistling down a track or a person flying down a slope on skis, but it is a good atmospheric device and a subtle modeling method. It is a very accurate way of representing photographic tones and excellent for incidental detail like the bloom on a person's cheek or a mark on their clothes.

The process of filling areas of your drawing with stippled marks is time-consuming and can be very tedious if you have to cover large areas. But avoid working too methodically. If you start at the outline and stipple consistently around a shape, the dots tend to make linear patterns. Put down an open field of random marks all over the shape; where you see gaps, start to fill them; then you see smaller gaps, which you can fill, and so on. That way the tones blend naturally and you can create tonal gradations by leaving some areas relatively open and filling others more densely.

FURTHER INFORMATION

Hatching, pages 80–81
Light & Shade, pages 86–87

Texture
Stippling is an excellent method for imitating certain textures, but remember that you need to build up the forms as well, so take care not to stipple evenly all over the drawing.

▲ A quick method of stippling is to use a stencil brush, or a bristle brush with the hairs splayed out. Use the minimum of paint or ink on the brush.

Rough stippling

1 This technique is good for rugged characters. Draw it in pencil or non-repro blue first, then start dashing in short pen strokes in dark shadow areas, roughly following the same direction.

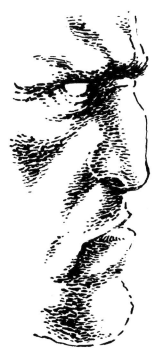

2 Work down the drawing, then go back and overwork the darkest tones. Leave the ink outline until last.

Mottled stipple

When the stippled marks are drawn out into short lines, the result is similar to shading.

Fine stippling

This technique has a very gradual build-up, so it is advisable to know what you are aiming for. Make a pencil sketch as a guideline (below) to decide how to treat different areas of the image. Here the artist has used gray paper for the sketch to act as a mid-tone, with hatched shading in pencil and highlighting in white crayon.

1 Lay in rough line work to form the basic structure. Keep the drawing minimal at this stage, so you do not pre-judge the tonal balance.

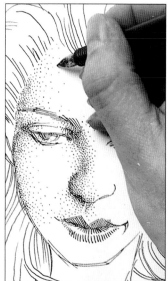

2 Block in the main areas of shadow with tiny dots made with the very tip of the pen. Space them more closely in deep shadows such as around eyes, nose, and chin, but keep the texture very open to begin with.

3 Go back over the whole shape, reworking the stippling to build up density of tone and strengthen the form. Try to keep the dots fine and separate so the texture does not fill in to solid black, but work closely to develop dark tones.

4 Repeat the process of stippling all over the drawing, making the dot pattern more dense where you see any rough gaps, but preserving highlight areas. The halo of dark hair, added with drybrushing, helps to emphasize the smoothly stippled tone.

The strip cartoon, or comic strip, is a long-established tradition of cartooning, but its status and presentation have been changing. Strips now vary from three-frame newspaper funnies, which are essentially throwaway items, to up to 96 pages of narrative in picture-strip form, in what has become known as "the graphic novel."

A major difference between the strip and the one-shot cartoon is that the strip includes the element of time. You can develop the idea of a strip sequence simply by writing down some basic aspect of your life – your background, such as where you were born and who your parents were; or a mundane action that you perform day-to-day, like peeling a potato – and then focusing on the important details which you could visualize in a few pictures. If you find it intimidating to work on it as a sequence of images, do them singly and paste them together to see how they work. The usual organization is multiples of three images, arranged in tiers.

Strips are not illustrations to a story; the visual and verbal elements are tightly knit in a kind of to-and-fro dance between them; one doesn't work without the other. As with single gags, you need to find the active moments in the story: what is exciting and what is not; what needs emphasis or not; who does what to whom. The narrative has subjects and objects, and in a developing sequence it is very important to make these relationships simple and striking.

One aspect of this is keeping your characters absolutely recognizable, whether they are seen in close-up or in background action. As you develop strip characters, draw them every way you can think of, until you know that person inside out and upside down. Because strips are unfolding in time like a movie, but have no real movement or sound, you may need to employ any number of cartoon conventions to "animate" your story.

Words feature largely in strips, and deciding how they function is part of the overall styling and character of your idea. Do you need captions underneath, as well as dialogue in the frame? Or do caption and commentary fit within the image? Make sure you keep to the basic principle of immediate impact and explanation – don't complicate matters for your reader.

If you are looking for a long-term commission for a strip, remember that it may run for many years, using three or more frames a day. A one-joke

Anatomy of a comic strip page

▼ A comic strip page is a series of juxtaposed panels, the components of which are anatomized here, showing how each combines to make up the page.

The panel is one complete division of a full sequence; it contains picture, word balloons, captions, sound effects, everything including the outline border

The space between panels is called the "gutter." Sometimes this can be no more than a simple dividing line

The picture is usually the major area of a panel and may extend across all of it

The caption usually contains third-person narration in a rectangular box

The word balloon carries dialogue or thought and is linked back to the picture by a "tail" or a row of ellipses

The sound effect is a bold, onomatopoeic word near the source of the sound for which it provides a calligraphic equivalent

idea simply won't sustain the exposure; you have to create characters and situations that can change and develop, or be used in a variety of ways. A strip cartoonist works like a novelist or playwright rather than a type of visual stand-up comic. Some people prefer to specialize in either story or pictures; but you are in the strongest position if you can be both author and artist. In practical terms, if you get a strip taken for publication, you may be asked to supply batches that keep your publisher a month ahead – it's a lot of work, but deadlines are all-important. On comic books, there may be vast numbers of people working on different aspects of the same visualization, just because the timing is so tight.

Characterization

Characters in strips function like characters in a movie or play. They are a cast: a group of figures held together by the traits which simultaneously distinguish them visibly from one another. Drawing them, you play a role similar to that of a casting director.

▲ The "cast" of characters is clearly defined. This is a group of uniformed police officers: visually, a group of uniforms with different heads on top. The distinctions between each figure are reduced to shape and tone of hairstyle, facial features, and decoration of uniforms.

▲ Comic strips in daily newspapers are usually allotted only part of a page. Such strips can be just a single row, or "tier" of three or four panels.

This is eminently suited to the gag strip. In this sort of format, you use the first panels to set up the gag and put the punchline in the last panel.

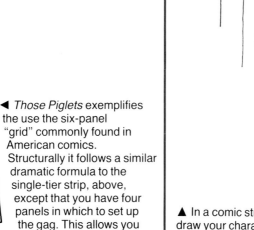

◀ *Those Piglets* exemplifies the use the six-panel "grid" commonly found in American comics.
Structurally it follows a similar dramatic formula to the single-tier strip, above, except that you have four panels in which to set up the gag. This allows you more interplay between characters.

▲ In a comic strip you must draw your characters many times from many angles. From the outset, you must have a mental picture of your "cast" in three dimensions. A good tip is to draw a model sheet for each character.

The breakdown

Whether you have just two panels or many pages to fill with your strip, the first stage in its construction is the rough breakdown. Some cartoonists prefer to pencil out "thumbnail" sketches at a fraction of the finished artwork's size. Others compose their sequences at the size their finished art will be reproduced. Either way the aim is the same: taking a scripted or merely visualized continuous sequence, you literally break it down into the picture, word balloon viewpoints, or sound-effect shapes which best carry the narrative. Below and right, gag and continuity breakdowns are explained.

STRIP ONE:

> POLICE BRUTALITY THAT'S WHAT THIS IS—

> A CLEAN WARM CELL—COLOURED TELEVISION

> THREE MEALS A DAY— HOT COCOA AND A BED AT NIGHT

> —AND NOW YOU TELL ME I'M FREE TO GO!

STRIP TWO:

> EMPTY YOUR POCKETS...

> ONE PACK OF CARDS, ONE BUNCH OF FLOWERS...

> TWO DOVES, ONE WHITE RABBIT—

> YOU COULD HAVE SAID YOU WERE A MAGICIAN!

▲ The less space you have, the tighter your scripting must be. Some gag cartoonists script their strips by writing dialogue in balloons, so that they can fine-tune their "payoff" lines. Such strips are usually scripted in batches of a week or more, depending on how far ahead your strip allows you to be.

▼ The development of a page from roughs to finished pencil is set out in three stages. The page is broken down from a script which will have been sent to the artist by an editor or the scriptwriter, with panels numbered and picture, action, and dialogue described.

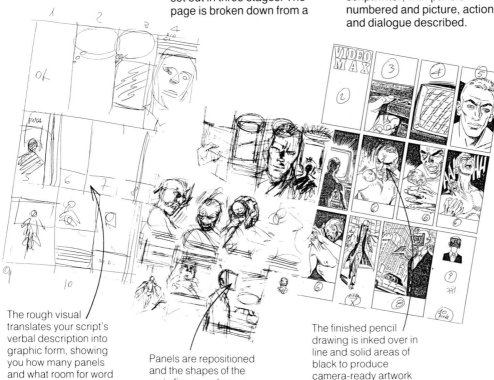

The rough visual translates your script's verbal description into graphic form, showing you how many panels and what room for word balloons you will need

Panels are repositioned and the shapes of the main figure and props are worked out in pencil.

The finished pencil drawing is inked over in line and solid areas of black to produce camera-ready artwork

Clichés and conventions

A cover may introduce characters and set the tone of the narrative. Similarly, the splash page is a convention which starts a strip with title, logo, credits, and a large or full-page picture which can be either any dramatic highlight from the plot or the first page of the narrative.

◀▶ In children's comics, above left, you may incorporate the distinctive attribute of a character graphically into the title, and make it part of the character's name. In a more realistic strip, left, you might use the title to familiarize the reader with the main character and important narrative elements. Right, the title is the name of the leading characters.

◀▶ The sort of picture you might use in an "establishing" panel. It suggests an outdoors scene, a sunny atmosphere, and a past period. All figures are shown at medium distance. Right, panel six establishes the position of characters sitting around a dinner table, so that panel 7 can feature a close view of the sinister Mr Moodus with surplus details omitted.

▲ All through this strip, the artist has packed in as much information as possible to build a sense of place and person. In panel three, the conversation between the children is indicated by speech balloons pointing to the front of a house, siting it in relation to a cemetery. This is followed by a close view of the two girls that registers little more than their expressions.

▼▶ The close-ups in this moody page exemplify one of comics' most characteristic devices: metonymy is 'where an attribute stands for the thing meant'; part for whole (and v/versa) is synecdoche. Top left, the black mass is a shadowy figure across a desk from a fat man. Top right, the fat man's vulgar necktie is indicative of its wearer's vulgarity. Bottom right, the reader knows that this is the fat man's hand because it extends out of the picture opposite to the shadowy, hatted face in panel four. Below, you can also use the close-up to introduce a new character

◀▲ The background to an overhead view grounds your figures and shows the layout of a scene. It is a classic "establishing" image, supplying general details of location or time.

◀ The pictures in most comic strip panels contain three-quarter views, usually in combination with other types of view, as here in panel three. Such images include general detail of features which you may have to leave out of an establishing picture or a close-up.

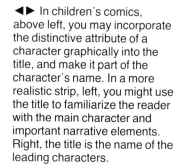

Pictorial depth

Three panels of a humor strip are enlarged and studied in detail for what they reveal about the way in which the conventions of pictorial depth function in strip sequences.

▲ There are differences at all depths of the picture. The path's direction has altered. The figures are larger in the midground: they are approaching. Retrospectively this indicates forward movement in panel one.

▲ Characters are in the midground, in the act of walking. The background establishes a light, fantasy setting. The sweep of the path recedes behind them and describes the direction from which they have walked. No message confirms whether or not they are approaching. For this, we will have to refer to the next panel.

▲ The characters are larger still, and almost in the foreground. Here they encounter the foreground figure. The background has also changed to show less detail; to continue with the same amount in this panel will make the picture too cluttered.

Transitions

The kinds of transitions you can make in a comic strip are as varied as any format will allow your drawings to be. The illustrations on this page include some of the most typical types of transitions to be found in the formats of gag and continuity strips.

▶ Alter very little between panels and you can focus on minutiae. The positions of the foreground figure in bed, and the layout of the background, remain constant. This strip is about the changing of the foreground character's expression from alarm to horror as another character arrives at the door.

▲ Position the caption at the top of each panel and the reader uses it first to interpret the scene. It gains the status of a TV voiceover. By slowly altering the viewpoint, you can play the framing of the panel border against the notional cinematic frame of a camera shutter. Here, the panel transitions imply the horizontal movement of a camera pan.

▲ Choosing the moment of action to illustrate is crucial. Look at what the reader isn't shown by the pictures in these panels. There's no image of the second figure bracing his arms and legs to strike the first.

There's no image of the first figure falling or of the second turning to go. You make a whole sequence through the images you choose as its parts.

◀ Between panels two and three, and five and six, the backgrounds change completely, signifying differences in place or time. However, the figure of Rodney Crumpet is present in both two and three. In other words, his character has moved directly from one location to the other and the surreal façade of Vulpine Villas replaces the relatively undistinctive interior of panels one and two. In the scene-change between panels five and six, there is no continuity of figures. With this type of scene-change, your reader won't expect a consequence: as if, in this example, Rodney were about to burst in and take his cattle-prod.

Layouts

If there is a rule in comic strip layout, it's that the more space you have, the more you do with it. In the case of a one-tier strip, your main job is to decide how you are going to put the panels next to each other. For a strip sequence that runs over a page or more, the structure of the whole page becomes integral to the storytelling process. On this page are five sequences showing different relations of panels in tiers and in the overall page layout of a story strip.

▼ This layout follows the pattern of a uniform grid. The viewpoint and very sparse background change negligibly, concentrating the reader's attention on the anthropomorphic insect.

▶ This single-tier strip solves the space problem of the gag cartoonist by reducing the content to a simple exchange. Essentially the same but for the different animated gestures that make up the anthropomorphic dog's reply, the three center panels are crucial to the gag's set-up.

▶ In contrast to the above, this gag strip follows a more conventional layout. The first, and biggest, panel contains an establishing picture with details of setting necessary for the gag: desert, sun, sweltering heat, gas station. This is followed by the gag itself: question in panel two and answer in panel three.

▼ Images introducing each main participant, plus a logo, are followed by a long, three-quarter view of the train with silhouettes picking out the relative positions. This is a title sequence but it has integrated into itself elements of the story.

MR. and MRS. R.V. RHODES

▼ These panels are decidedly non-standard in shape, size, and design. The L-shape of the large panel dominates the lay-out by surrounding the outline of the diving figure. The curved panel shapes create gutters which suggest waves.

The effects used to denote body movement are carried over, linking the insect in panel eleven with the box in panel twelve

Words

There are three principal types of verbal ingredient in comic strips. Word balloons contain thought and dialogue. Captions include first or third person narration. Sound effects render sonic forms phonetically. The examples here all acknowledge the "gravity" of strip reading in which everything is scanned like the sequence of panels on a page: from left to right and from top to bottom.

▶ This strip sequence shows the figure of a little girl in a matador costume riding a rocking horse. In panel one, JEEOOP!, separated from the picture space by a jagged balloon, is read before the repeated CRICKETY CRACK of the horse being rocked. Note how the sound effect lettering works in the pictorial space of a panel. Effect lettering can be cropped by the panel border just like elements of the picture.

▲ Running narration beneath a panel border is an archaic comic technique. You can use it ironically, as here, to evoke an old-fashioned "voice." Unlike above right, sound effects and balloons are crisply contained inside the picture area. In panel four, a speech balloon is placed, as if it were an effect, on the floor to indicate dialogue from the shadow of The Penguin's unseen figure.

▼ Where you position extensive dialogue in a strip, you must bear in mind the order in which balloons will be read. Quite complex arrangements can emerge, such as the split balloon in panel three which, in order to pose a question, shapes a part of the balloon border over the balloon containing the answer. Panels three and five show overlapping balloons, used here to ensure that dialogue does not mix.

Stages of production

On these two pages, the essential stages in the development of a comic strip are outlined using the example of a story written by Alan McKenzie and drawn by Steve Parkhouse. It uses the model favored in the production of some comics, where writers approach publishers with an idea independently of an artist. If the idea is acceptable to an editor, the script will be accepted on its own merits.

▶ The script is laid out in a standard format listing panel number, picture description, captions, dialogue, thought or sound effects. This method puts some onus on the writer to break down a sequence visually. Another popular method is to describe the action that takes place on a page, to pass this to an artist, and to write the definitive script later.

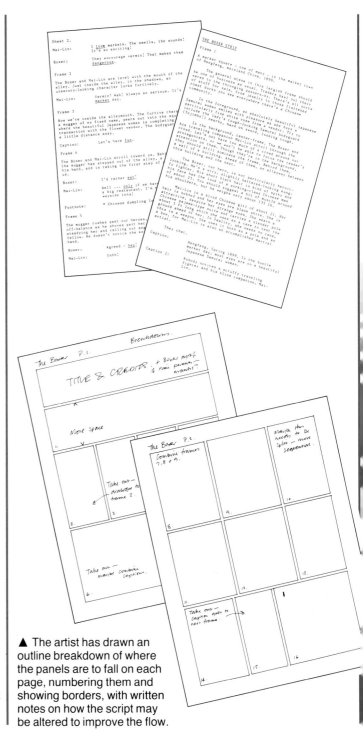

▲ Before laying out pages you can draw a model sheet of characters, so that you know what they look like from various angles, in postures and in appropriate costumes. Sometimes this process is referred to as "character design." If the characters are to be in a series, they may be drawn from descriptions in the writer's story proposal, before a word of the first episode is scripted.

▲ The artist has drawn an outline breakdown of where the panels are to fall on each page, numbering them and showing borders, with written notes on how the script may be altered to improve the flow.

▲ The pencil stage. More detail is required if you are passing this to an inker than if you are inking it yourself.

▼ At the ink stage, all lines and black areas must be clear, however loosely they are drawn.

▲ Final artwork includes the captions and balloons. For line artwork, as here, lettering is drawn on patch-paper and stuck directly on the inked page.

For artwork that is in full color, lettering is positioned on an acetate overlay with registration marks to ensure that nothing slips out of place.

VIEWPOINT

A cartoon can be treated as a picture of something happening one step away from the viewer, or you can draw your audience into the frame, almost as participants in the action. Similarly, the viewers' sympathy and association with the characters and events within the cartoon can be to some extent directed by the cartoonist, by organizing the composition in a way that suggests how they should see it, not just what they see.

Take the example of an encounter with the potential for conflict – an argument between a married couple, or employer and employee; two gunfighters facing each other, or a pair of animals squaring up for a spat. If you just show these characters centered within the frame, the viewer is an uninvolved onlooker and the situation seems equally weighted. To draw the viewer in, you could bring one of the protagonists right to the edge of the frame, seeing the other beyond and as if from the first person's point of view. To suggest that the combatants are unequal, you could just make one of them taller, fatter, more muscle-bound; or you could give your viewer a worm's-eye view, so that the nearer contestant looks huge

and towering, while the other is distanced a little more and therefore appears in a relatively normal scale.

Some people have no trouble visualizing things from different angles, while others have to toil away with perspective guidelines and grids. But taking an unexpected viewpoint can give much greater impact to your cartoon, underlining the point or inserting a subversive commentary.

FURTHER INFORMATION

Backgrounds, pages 32–37
Foreshortening, pages 74–75
Perspective, pages 98–101

Viewpoint and impact
▲ This confrontation remains directly between the two protagonists: you as viewer watch it like a movie, from a comfortable distance. The characters are symmetrically positioned and equally defined in scale and detail.

▲ This dramatic and interesting angle puts the viewer in the line of fire. The figures overlap, but distance is created by accurate handling of tone and scale.

▼ The so-called "worm's-eye" or ground-level viewpoint literally heightens the drama. Here the shapes that create the leaning stance of the foreground figure, seen almost flat-on, are cleverly shadowed with thick black lines.

▼ Bird's-eye or fly-on-the-ceiling viewpoint explains the spatial relationship of figures well, but needs effective foreshortening to work convincingly.

▲ The way these figures are cut off by the frame in close view explains a huge difference in their heights. That part of the joke works without any caption.

▼ The character looming out of the frame, right in front of the viewer, gets the harder definition of heavyweight line.

123

HUMOR

The modern cartoon joke has evolved very freely since nineteenth-century magazines started to include humorous verse, prose, and drawings that became fashionable and popular. Old-style cartoons typically had a particular political or social point to make; often the drawing merely made a tableau and the joke was carried in a caption "conversation." Gradually, words and pictures became snappier and more immediate, and the drawing itself made the humor more explicit. Topical references were not essential, though often still used, as long as the cartoon was funny and likely to have broad appeal.

As film, television, and radio emphasized the element of comic timing in humorous dialogue, cartoon captions became clipped, often relying on the cartoonist's command of colloquialisms and exclamations. Words are now more directly integrated with pictures, and both are simplified to have an instant impact. But publishing and broadcasting media have also supplied a pool of shared reference that cartoonists can draw upon for ideas, images, language, and presentation.

There are certain subjects that have always lent themselves to cartooning – politics, class differences, and social hierarchies of all kinds, sexual manners, new inventions, public events. Animals have often featured, usually anthropomorphized to a high degree or representing the human condition. Cartoon humor often works by prodding at a natural conservatism in the audience, but cartoons need to make fun of people in a way that enables them to share the joke, so that the shaft of wit is pointed but not too personally cruel.

A sense of humor is not necessarily universal or even shared between friends and family, so it is no wonder that modern cartooning includes a vast range of ideas and interpretations. Throwaway newspaper cartoons endlessly recycle the humor of ordinary relationships between husbands and wives, parents and children, lovers, employers and employees – humor which is easily grasped by a wide audience. At the other end of the spectrum are cartoons that focus on a seemingly irrelevant element, taking the use of the unexpected as close to meaninglessness as the cartoonist dares.

It isn't easy to predict what will make a successful visual joke, or what will find favor with an editor's judgment. Sometimes off-the-wall humor starts as a minority preference, gets picked up as a cult, and eventually goes into the mainstream. As a cartoonist, you need to use, and trust, your own sense of humor to form a common thread through what you do.

"It was his last request. He wanted his ashes emptied down Charlie Cairoli's trousers."

▲ ALBERT
The black humor of this cartoon is associated with the commonly held notion that clowns are deeply sad people who hide their sorrow by clowning. The composition and tonality of the ink line-and-wash drawing emphasize the funereal nature of the joke, with the sooty black background hanging in a heavy pall over the stooped figures. The clowns and ringmaster are portrayed as stereotypes, with traditional clothes and circus make-up, but the artist has introduced subtle variations of shape and form that give each a sense of individuality.

"It's a portable one-man desk top publishing unit."

▲ BANX

The artist uses an uncluttered style, contrasting simple line drawing with areas of solid black, so that the detail of the main figure and his invention is clearly stated. But there is a dancing rhythm in the black shapes that leads the eye easily through the image.

"Look on the bright side, at least you've discovered a cure for baldness."

◄ MIKE WILLIAMS

Pen lines, colored ink washes, and chalk drawing give an attractive painterly quality to this limited edition cartoon. The bold color composition is anchored by a strong zigzag framework traveling through the picture, from the door to the woman, along her sightline to the wolf-man, and from his face into the foreground. The scenario is familiar horror-movie imagery that focuses the punchline by its contrast of bizarre and everyday elements.

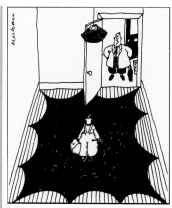

"Well it's not MY idea of wall-to-wall carpets."

▲ MEEHAN

The idea for this cartoon has suggested the point of view – it is essential to see the whole floor, so a high viewpoint is naturally established. The shrinking carpet makes a dynamic black shape, well combined with minimal linear detail which frames the central focus.

"If I may say so, my Lord, you are not only a superb shot, but a man of taste and discrimination."

◀ ROLAND FIDDY
The open, economical drawing style of the cartoon provides the basic setting of a spacious stately home. In this relatively featureless environment, the butler is the focus of almost all the detail, so that you immediately look to him for the point of the gag.

▲ KARL DIXON
This episodic image keeps control over its series of random but related events by placing the figures and objects within a simple box-like construction. The limited color scheme of transparent ink washes has a broadly descriptive as well as decorative function.

◀ HALDANE
The picture is divided diagonally with all the important information falling within the left-hand section. The diagonal leads directly from the central figure to the two figures watching him in the background. Surrounding incidental detail has a uniform style based on wavy lines and washes of mid-toned grays. The artist gives a humorous twist to a classic myth from the King Arthur legend which is assumed to be familiar to the audience for the cartoon.

▶ PAT DRENNAN
Like the King Arthur cartoon (below left), this drawing takes a well-known story and alters the outcome to create a joke. The broad horizontal format is exploited with an even spread of activity moving across the width of the drawing as the story unfolds from left to right, but there are distinct vertical and diagonal stresses that give a lively rhythm to the image. Varying line qualities and grades of tone emphasize form and depth.

▼ MIKE WILLIAMS
The viewer's attention travels against the implied momentum of this drawing, going left to right toward the occupants of the car who furnish the punchline. The line work and washes are vigorously applied and left free. The cartoon would be ruined by a conventional rectangular frame.

"Parkinson! For Heaven's sake, man, stop or we'll all be killed!"

"I hate these sudden-death playoffs."

◄ MEYRICK JONES
In this very simple line drawing the relationship of the figures indicates a sense of space; the setting is absolutely minimal. In printing, the drawing was given body with dropped-in tone not originally indicated by the artist.

► MACLACHAN
The shading on the background and all the staring heads of the students line up with the swish of the decapitation. The background of simple verticals and two circular motifs anchors the drawing without reference to a floor or ceiling or any form of perspective. The master's black belt, the only solid black in the image, serves to emphasize his importance. The artist has made the most of individual facial expressions to underline the grotesque humor of the gag.

"The discipline at this club has always been very strict."

▶ MARTY MURPHY
All the detail in this drawing makes the naked figures stand out, and also gives a wry commentary, as the trophies and pictures help to establish the self-importance and golfing obsession of the cuckolded husband. The basic perspective applied to the shapes of the furniture leads the eye toward the background figure.

". . . It's my husband! Damn! He must have missed the cut!"

◀ SAX
The central joke is focused in a classic triangular composition, formed by the attitudes of the discus thrower and the shouting official. The athlete's posture is based on a classical pose seen in ancient statuary, its potential elegance contrasted with his apparent crudity. Following the triangular outline of the main figures, you find some secondary jokes about javelin-throwing supplementing the action. The color work is drawn with broad markers, and their linear strokes add to the energy of the image.

"Ancient Greeks or not. Put your shorts on!"

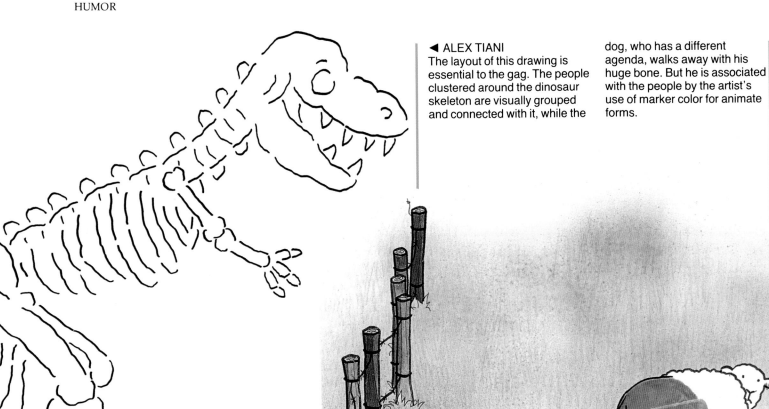

◄ ALEX TIANI
The layout of this drawing is essential to the gag. The people clustered around the dinosaur skeleton are visually grouped and connected with it, while the dog, who has a different agenda, walks away with his huge bone. But he is associated with the people by the artist's use of marker color for animate forms.

▲ CLIVE COLLINS
This color cartoon makes clever use of the "negative" white line contrasting with the black keyline drawing and bright gouache color. It attracts the eye and leads into the joke. Despite the open outline and relative simplicity of the setting, careful drawing of the fence establishes both depth and point of view. The grassy texture is marker strokes overlaid with wash, leaving residual lines.

► CLIVE COLLINS
The artist has used both pen texture and tonal wash to pull the wolves into the foreground, leaving the background treatment as simple washed silhouettes. The shape of the drawing is important; with the open outline, it takes a moment to realize that the comfortable "living room" is a cave.

"Good heavens, is that the time? I really must go and bay at the moon . . ."

◄ CRAMER
The props in this image are essential to the joke – the sign marking the sushi bar and the fact that the dog is eating with chopsticks. The cartoon is focused just off-center, where the drawing is most detailed and vigorous. On either side, the line work is more open, and dropped-in mechanical tone highlights the focal points.

The word "cartoon" as we use it today was first applied to satirical drawings rather than simply humorous ones. The satire relied on the reader being familiar with a social or political situation that the artist could make ridiculous by exaggerating it or presenting it in an unflattering way.

The direct modern descendant of this tradition is the editorial cartoon that forms a major feature in a daily newspaper. The cartoonist's comment on an important national or international event accompanies or complements the editorial commentary. These often include direct caricatures of politicians or other people involved whose faces have become well known through the story. They may use symbols, stereotypes, or allegory to parody the event, while ensuring that the topical reference is clear.

Satire is, however, one of the most common forms of humor in the modern world, easily applied to all kinds of subject matter that is widely recognized and understood. The media are self-satirizing to a great extent – many cartoons relate to the content and presentation of television and movies, for example. Details of politics, law, religion, and social customs broadly known to readers of newspapers and magazines can become targets of humor at any time, even when not immediately in the news.

Cartoons can use an economical and oblique "language" to carry large ideas. The satirical comment can act for or against the main idea, either promoting or criticizing attitudes to, say, green issues, feminist thought, or political correctness. Cartoons are often regarded as throwaway comment and few outlast the direct context, but occasionally the immediacy of a cartoon can make considerable impact. If the cartoonist gets the message and the visual encapsulation of it just right, a cartoon can form a memorable icon of events.

▶ STEVE WAY
Television provides a common pool of reference that cartoonists can draw on for humor and comment. Here the late hour is directly stated by the caption on screen, the dark window, and the character's lazy gesture, and quietly underscored by the use of loose hatching to create tone, which gives the shapes a slightly unformed, shadowy quality. Focal points are brought out by the absence of tone on the face and television.

"Wait a minute – he's got the drunken preacher, the grizzled old-timer, and the callow youth; it's the complete Western cliché; we don't stand a chance."

▲ PAUL LOWE
This cartoon satirizes the use of movie stereotypes in an affectionate way. Sketchy, bold ink drawing gives a gritty feel well suited to the subject. Although detail is minimal and the figures lack a formal setting, location and mood are strongly implied. The balance of black and white is excellently handled, with the long shadows closing the gap between the individuals and the crowd.

▲ HUNT EMERSON
This drawing was made for exhibition at a festival of cartooning with an Olympic theme. Each section of the picture has its own joke and point of view, but the incidents have been visually linked so they occupy the page as if following an athletics course. However, the makeshift "course" doubles the athletes' effort, as everyone is being carried by somebody else. Not only facial features but every aspect of the body language and gestures has been devised to add emphasis and expression, distorting or simplifying as appropriate – note that all the characters have the economical, three-fingered cartoon hand. The faces highlight the humor – the usual grim concentration of athletes is here and there replaced by aggression, anxiety, resignation, and beatific ease.

▲ BRIAN BOLLAND
Homage to other artists' work enables a cartoonist to introduce a range of references that comment on the story. This comic book cover condenses the composition of *The Nightmare* by eighteenth-century painter Henry Fuseli and reinterprets the symbolic figures in a modern context. Rich tonal contrasts and controlled hatching create a beautiful interplay of open and detailed forms.

"I've been granted visiting rights, but only to 150 of them."

◄ LONG
The subject of a topical cartoon is usually a matter for serious debate in the real world. Here the concentrated effort which the police put into testing their billies satirically mirrors concern over the use of weapons in law enforcement. The pen drawing is simple and lively, framing the notice which also acts as the cartoon caption.

◄ CLIVE COLLINS
This cartoon is a comment on the disintegration of family life, interpreted through the frogs looking cold-bloodedly at the hundreds of anonymous spawn. It is also a mood piece in which the well-styled marker drawing and smooth washes of color help to emphasize the sense of isolation and absurdity.

► DON ROBERTS
This is a nice use of dry shading to give body to the pen drawing. As the ink line work is fairly loose, the dry shading becomes the complexion of the drawing, holding it together as you "read" the situation and detail. There is a kind of solid realism to the main image gently subverted by the tiny caricatures of stranded animals taking to the boats.

"Bad news, dear, the drought relief scheme's become a victim of the spending cuts."

137

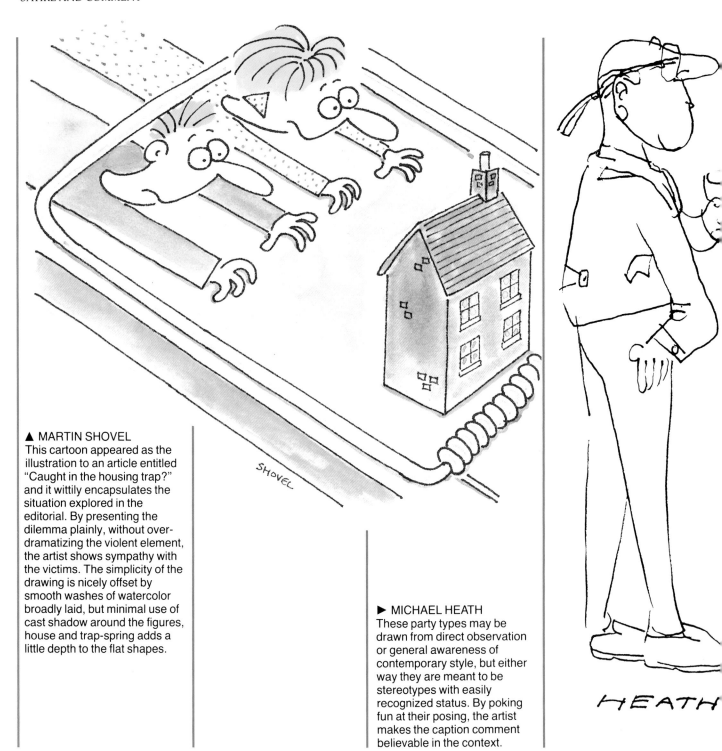

▲ MARTIN SHOVEL
This cartoon appeared as the illustration to an article entitled "Caught in the housing trap?" and it wittily encapsulates the situation explored in the editorial. By presenting the dilemma plainly, without over-dramatizing the violent element, the artist shows sympathy with the victims. The simplicity of the drawing is nicely offset by smooth washes of watercolor broadly laid, but minimal use of cast shadow around the figures, house and trap-spring adds a little depth to the flat shapes.

▶ MICHAEL HEATH
These party types may be drawn from direct observation or general awareness of contemporary style, but either way they are meant to be stereotypes with easily recognized status. By poking fun at their posing, the artist makes the caption comment believable in the context.

"It's not what you think - I'm only here with her because she can work the video recorder."

"Can you tell me the time please, constable?"

▲ DE LA NOUGEREDE
The situation is wholly conveyed in the figure poses, moving from the concentration of the left-hand figure to the distracted marksman, to the elderly lady apparently oblivious to the unseen drama. There is a nice use of black, loosely brushed into the pen drawing.

▼ BILL CALDWELL
The Pope is brightly lit among his shadowy entourage and the aisles of the stadium radiate from his central figure. With the solid blacks in the foreground and open line work in the background, this creates a clear sense of perspective and depth. The drawing and caption are perfectly complementary.

"A big welcome to my non-gay, non-divorced, no-drugs flock in California."

SORRY, I FEEL REALLY BAD ABOUT THIS

"It's a new, environmentally friendly chainsaw."

▲ HALDANE
Sting-in-the-tail humor works on successive levels. This cartoon makes a sharp observation on how ecological awareness has become required thinking, but has a bitter subtext on the hypocrisy of taking inadequate measures to improve the situation. The line-and-wash drawing in restricted tonal range shows the artist's distinctive style.

▶ WILSON
The crayon drawing creates softened line and tone, contrasting with the harsh message of the cartoon. The grainy shading draws attention to the passengers, their sight-lines and surroundings, and on to the bulletin board caption.

WELCOME TO FLORIDA THE SUNSHINE STATE IT ONLY RAINS BULLETS.

▼ LARRY

Cartoons often play a role in advertising, as in this example from a book of cartoons commissioned by JCB. All the attention is focused on the "Swiss army knife" vehicle, which carries the company's logo, and the directions of lines, shading, and figurative content lead back to it. The vehicle itself is an intriguing, witty creation, and the surrounding craziness makes the cartoon even funnier.

▶ HUGO PRATT

The astronaut discovering new moons to conquer provides a narrative suggestion open to various interpretations. This personal statement by the artist makes a lovely, balanced color image despite the economy of means. Delicate line-and-wash work stands out against the rich, velvety black. The shape of the spaceman's helmet cleverly echoes the crescent forms in the background almost like another moon, so that he is part of his surroundings as well as an alien presence.

you may call me old fashioned....

I didn't, I called you an obstructive opinionated sexist bigot.

JF

► JACKY FLEMING
The subject of this cartoon is anger, and it is expressed through every aspect of the drawing: the visual immediacy of the slanted brows and bared teeth; the implied tension of body and arms, and the manic scribble representing the hair.

►► JACKY FLEMING
Because we are used to such glamorous stereotypes, the message of the caption is at first merely amusing; then the grotesqueness of the idea kicks in as quite a shock. Most cartoon imagery is designed to be easily assimilable, but in this case it sticks in the mind and unravels layers of implication.

Men's brains are heavier than women's brains!

▲ JACKY FLEMING
All of the cartoons on this page dealing with feminist issues represent the way this field of communication can carry serious and large ideas to the widest possible audience. A common feature of such cartoons is a relative lack of detail; captions are important, and the reader is required to think on and see the broader picture. Despite the simplicity of the drawing, a distinct personal style emerges. In Jacky Fleming's work, the open, fluid pen drawing constructs a clear sense of the characters and their social relationship. Their postures are wonderfully descriptive of each person's role and attitude. To a degree, they are stereotypes, but also come across as real people that the reader will have encountered in similar situations.

► ANNIE LAWSON
This artist's pen-and-ink line drawing reduces characters to the most minimal, essential forms that allow recognition. The use of stick figures is a clever way of stating social commentary regardless of individual input, because we are not able to make assumptions about who these people are or why they relate to each other in this way. She has used basic codes of facial expression on which the reader can project the response.

Why can't you be NICE to me when I've got PMS?

I found this fabulous little man who just moved my buttocks round to the front. So simple.

▼ RIANA DUNCAN
A comment on some men's attitude to women in the workplace. This cartoon has no borders, conveying an impression of a spacious boardroom. Miss Triggs is cut off from the rest of the board members by the verticals of the door, accentuating the chairman's disregard for her worth.

"That's an excellent suggestion, Miss Triggs. Perhaps one of the men here would like to make it."

► MEEHAN

A funny, childish situation reveals a shocking truth about violence and power. The children's game of snap – a random matching of picture cards – represents an arbitrary element in the seizure of Native Americans' territories, and the image also satirizes past movie conventions that cast cowboys as winners and Indians as losers. The artist uses uniform line work to state the picture simply, adding a little texture to enliven the characterizations. Notice the device of using tiny, fragile lines to denote hand movements.

HOW THE WEST WAS WON.

◄ ARNOLD ROTH

Santa Claus bearing gifts and being made welcome is a familiar image, but this vision of former President Ronald Reagan bearing a sack full of nuclear weapons and sprinkling fake snow in the desert is a disturbing and sinister one. Roth's beautiful dip-pen work is complemented by superbly atmospheric watercolor blurring the desert horizon into the domes and minarets in the distant haze. Tonally, everything that needs to be noticed comes forward and draws the eye.

> THEY LEFT THIS CHAP BEHIND TO OBSERVE THE FIGHTING.

SARAJEVO

▲ CLIVE WAKFER
This image uses drawing devices more typically associated with comic books than with one-shot cartoons, as if it were a single frame isolated from the action, which is one point of the commentary. The semi-realistic figures are described by harshly hatched lines, while the menacing death figure has a rough, explosive white-on-black drybrushed texture surrounded by coarse black spattering. It forms a central inverted triangle that implies giant proportions by breaking through the upper frame.

▶ ARTHUR REED
Focusing on ordinary people, this cartoon links hard facts of economic life in the former Soviet Union with the element of political uncertainty, but the seriousness of the message is subverted by the insouciant caption comment. The lively line work more than adequately sets the scene and characters.

"Is this the line for the presidency?"

It could be said that caricature is the most obvious form of cartooning. Other people have been readily available and continuously fascinating subjects for artists throughout the ages. No doubt there have always been humorously exaggerated portraits and figure drawings that gently or crudely move beyond an ordinary representation.

However, caricature is possibly also the hardest cartoon type to master. It is not just a question of any old funny drawing of a famous face, but a matter of appropriateness, capturing a commonly held impression of the person you are caricaturing. You need a certain courage, or even ruthlessness, if you decide to become a caricaturist; you have to be prepared to assume an attitude of merciless dissatisfaction and learn to hold up an acutely partial magnifying glass to your subject's features.

A caricature is often, in simple terms, an unkind view, because the features most easy to exaggerate may also be those the subject might be personally sensitive about. This could be inhibiting if you start practicing on drawings of friends and family, and you

may also find it difficult to take a coldly objective view of someone you know. But objectivity is essential and the caricaturist has to be able to apply it in a versatile way. A caricaturist representing politicians, actors, rock stars, and media personalities, or those people who just seem to be famous for being famous, must be ready to work on anyone who suddenly makes news or is sought after – and also be prepared to drop a well-honed caricature when its subject no longer commands the atttention he or she once did.

As a topical branch of cartooning, caricature is subject to visual fashions. It is not always enough to get at the subject accurately; sometimes the success of a caricaturist depends on having presented the drawing itself in a style that also catches the mood of the time and background context. Although you can pick up tips on style and technique from established artists, remember that the better they are known, the more their influence on you may be obvious. Inexpensive imitators of famous cartoonists are sometimes in demand and most fashions produce a short-lived bandwagon effect, but this can also count against your work. So make a real effort to use the ideas that you pick up to produce something clearly your own.

◄ CAMLEY
This caricature of British Prime Minister John Major, "The Nation Awaits," refers to his delay on setting a date for the 1992 general election. The circus background refers to his trapezist father. The figure is spotlit within a cone of light masked off from a coarsely spattered background. The eyeglasses' blank gaze shows indecision and Major's most notable physical feature, his long upper lip, is vastly exaggerated.

► "GAL"
This complex double portrait of Stalin and Hitler is executed in mixed media, including pastel, colored pencil, and charcoal with a laid-in color film background. By spotting certain physical similarities between two of the twentieth century's most ruthless dictators, the artist has achieved a believable composite which signifies the political similarities between these apparent enemies in their exercise of power.

◄ EMMS
This image is a kind of dual caricature: Russia itself is represented in the symbolic form of the bear, which both threatens Boris Yeltsin and depends on him to nurture democracy. Yeltsin's heavy features are shown with minimum exaggeration. In keeping with the style, the tonal drawing is descriptive, though the grays are hatched rather than washed in to avoid the need for halftone reproduction.

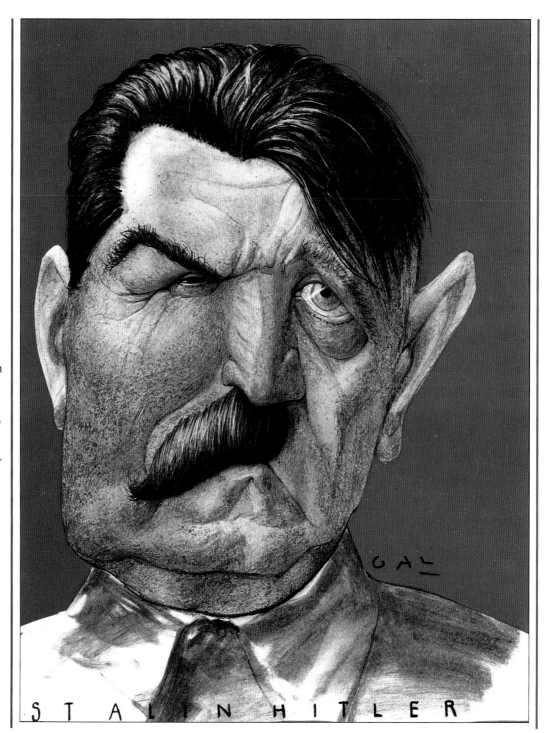

STALIN HITLER

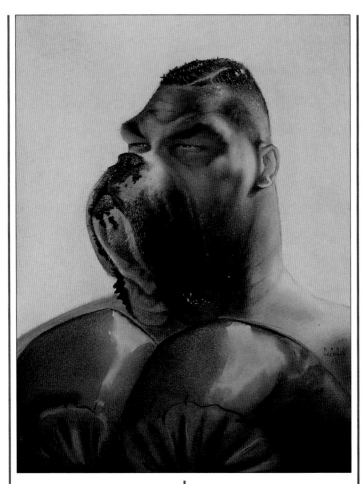

▲ KARL MEERSHAN
Here is a simple visual pun –
the face of an infamous boxer
which merges with that of a
boxer dog. The face is carefully
rendered in hot flesh tones; the
foreground is cool with two
huge, blue-black boxing gloves.
Tyson's head has been
distorted to fit in with the dog
snout he's been given – all it
lacks is a pair of floppy ears.

▲ CARL FLINT
Not just a caricature but a
comment on Arnold
Schwarzenegger's status as a
movie star, involving many
visual puns and references to
his appearance as the
monstrous mechanical
assassin in the *Terminator*
movies. Flint has used collages
of Schwarzenegger's face –
suitably altered to accentuate
the "squarehead" haircut.

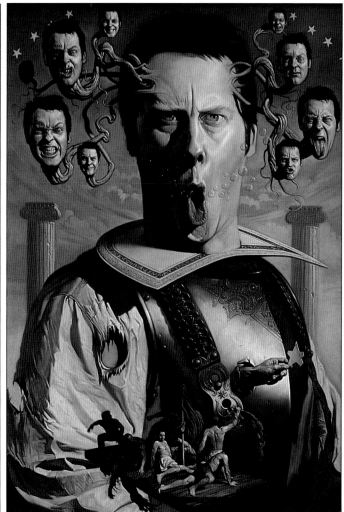

▲ BRIAN BOLLAND
This is closer to a conventional portrait than what we normally think of as a caricature. It was commissioned for the cover of an adventure comic featuring the pop star Prince (as the story's hero he could hardly be lampooned by its jacket). The portrait is in the artist's usual comic-strip style. The initial finely hatched black-and-white drawing was hand-colored to give a photographic quality to the figure. The cold colors on the jacket, hair, and gloves separate the hero from his fiery background, and an intensely bright yellow pushes the guitar forward. The hot and cold colors complement the black and white of the drawing.

▲ RICHARD DOLAN
The cartoonist is free to exploit any and all techniques: this oil painting, commissioned by the subject, reveals the artist's interest in and knowledge of post-Renaissance European portraiture. The artist worked from a photograph, but the highly realistic style, coupled with the disturbing fantasy, gives the painting a dreamlike, if not nightmarish, quality. It is reminiscent of the work of the Surrealists, notably Salvador Dali and the collagist, Max Ernst. A thorough examination of the technique of this painting would be an art education in itself.

149

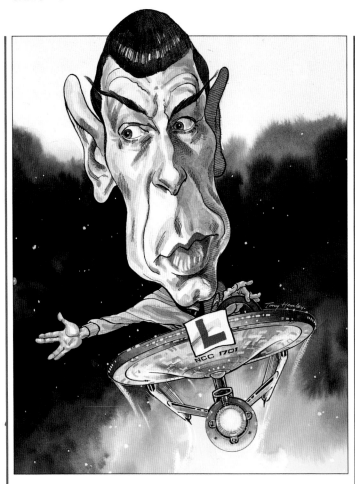

▲ TONY HEALEY
Popular television characters are more often caricatured than the actors who play them, but it is not enough to rely on features that are already exaggerated, such as Mr Spock's pointy ears. In this watercolor portrait, using ink line to hold the detail of the characterization, the artist has had to apply a logical, consistent distortion to all aspects of his subject.

▼ BRUNO
This portrait of a zombified rock'n'roller is identifiable but the caricature serves to make a general point about how an excessive lifestyle may sap energy and charm. Technically, the drawing is clever and stylishly done, using the delicate gradations of ink wash to suggest form and atmosphere.

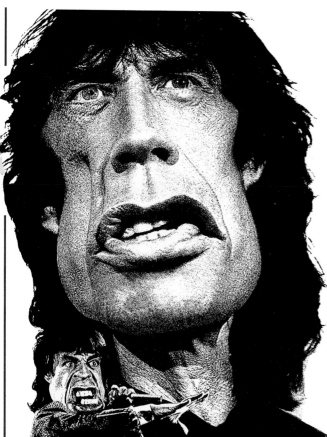

◀ PETER CLARKE
These caricatures of Mick Jagger and the Duchess of York are typical of this artist's use of computer functions to distort and exaggerate photographic data. Computerized image manipulation opens up a new order of technique for the cartoonist, because highly realistic detail can be directly applied to picture-making, but interpreted in imaginative and totally unrealistic ways.

PETER MADDOCKS
▼ It would be possible to leave out all the facial features but the beard from this drawing of opera singer Luciano Pavarotti, and let body shape, gesture, and the characteristic handkerchief prop identify the caricature.

PETER MADDOCKS
◀ A caricature must combine the actor's characteristic facial features with an image equally characteristic of the parts played. Here Bogart's high forehead, sloping brow, wrinkled bags, and 5 o'clock shadow, all join together in a face that sits atop a khaki trenchcoat which Bogart's roles made into the classic private dick's uniform.

Picture-strip stories have been around for about a century, beginning in much the same form that we know today. Newspapers and magazines ran single-tier or whole-page comic strips on a variety of subjects, based around families, individuals and, of course, animals acting like humans. Adventure and romance strips developed somewhat later, becoming the soap operas of their age and syndicated to newspapers around the world. Then came the three- or four-panel gag strip, providing a self-contained joke but with a running theme, context, and characters. Collections of previously published picture-stories were gathered into books and spawned the current concept of the graphic novel, with the concept wholly originated for publication in that form.

Strips have covered just about every literary and cinematic genre imaginable, provided straightforward laughs or wry running commentaries, and have even been used to dispense serious information, advice, and instructions in palatable form. You have only to look at the range that may be included in one weekend newspaper or supplement to see the variety of subject matter and style that is being applied to this form of cartooning. However, newspaper readerships are generally dwindling and the publication of syndicated strips in book form, or of original graphic novels, brings conventional treatments and developing ideas to a very wide audience.

Strips can revive history, comment on the world we live in, or invent whole new worlds for people to enter. They deal with abstract and surreal ideas as well as ongoing daily concerns – who does the dishes, who walks the dog, who averts the threat to humanity from outer space, who knows what we're all doing here anyway. From the sublime to the ridiculous, strips cover all the ground, and do so with increasingly inventive graphics. Techniques exploit all the standard forms of black-and-white communication, but many now command the extra impact of color printing throughout and can also explore new means of expression only loosely attached to standard comic book conventions.

▲ BRIAN BOLLAND
High-contrast lighting emphasizes the dynamics of this sequence. The hard-edged black-and-white areas linked by minimal, evenly hatched shading, create sharp focus. The tones are well balanced in each frame, and through the image as a whole. Lines and whole shapes reinforce the action, thrusting across horizontal frames for the most dynamic movement, while the verticals are like stills in the action sequence, particularly the upper left-hand frame, which relates to all three right-hand horizontals. This large portrait is lit from below, making the character more frightening and dominant, and the foreshortened hand breaking out of its frame aids the illusion of depth.

"HELLO.

"I CAME TO TALK."

◀ BRIAN BOLLAND
Reduced to the silhouetted shape of his cape and hood, Batman remains instantly recognizable but has a threatening presence. In the second frame, he is represented only by the tentacle-like folds of the cape, from which the figures in the background flee in terror. Clean definition and exactly judged contrasts of black-and-white emphasis create mood and narrative.

◀ DAVID LLOYD
The somber palette and textured watercolor washes have a gritty social realist style. Attention to clothes and props underscores the sense of naturalism, and the light sources are distinctive in each frame. Boxes are left for hand-lettered text to be dropped in.

▲ DAN SPIEGLE
The lit frames are shaded with varied weights of hatching, but a mechanical tint provides the evenly dark, nighttime effect at top left. Simultaneous events are indicated by the way the hand holding the grenade discreetly overlaps the image above.

▲ DAN SPIEGLE

A lot of the styling in this strip contributes directly to the period flavor. Although the drawing is relatively simplified to suit strip format, the detail creates a sense of realism. The extended background of the title frame sets the scene admirably, and the older character's clothing is immediately seen clearly enough to fix him in his own time. Consistent chiaroscuro lighting adds to the flavor of the piece, although the black-and-white contrasts are cleverly varied between positive and negative forms. The sequence is full of active texture denoting specific details, but the artist keeps visual control of the narrative throughout and the word balloons are kept clean. The device of occasionally bleeding off white shapes into the surrounding borders breaks the rigidity of framing, enhancing the flow of narrative. The inset cameo in the lower frame enables the artist to handle layers of information.

▲ BRIAN BOLLAND
The artist has used black as a focusing device in the first panel. Your eye goes straight to the rat's solid black shape. Conversely, in following panels the murderer is predominantly white, spotlit against dark windows that reflected mid-tones in the first frame. The murderer's actions are dramatically underlined with heavy cast shadows and movement lines for violent gestures. Part of the fascination lies in a switch of emphasis. In detailed scene-setting, the store fronts and windows reflecting opposite buildings are organized in faultless one-point perspective. Then the close focus, flat-on views of the characters involve the viewer directly.

▲ D'ISRAELI
A rework of the Snow White fairy tale, parodying popular stage and Disney versions, bizarrely inserts a male principal character and gives the narrative a sense of underlying threat. The drawing, by contrast, is simplified and sometimes deliberately charming, as in the frames showing the cottage and woodland animals, so the violent elements seem the more disturbing. The line work is consistent overall, with white lines reversed out of solid black shapes which give a sharp graphic feel, and occasional loose hatching to make mid-toned grays or convey specific textures such as grass or wood. The artist used pen and brush drawing over a page layout first drawn in blue pencil. Where corrections were needed after inking, they were scratched back with a razor blade.

◀ HUNT EMERSON
The backgrounds change surreally from frame to frame, but the artist knows your attention is on the main characters and the way they develop the gag. The spotted cat is always the focus, and has a strong outline to add emphasis, as do the other players in the story, the kittens and the disembodied arm. Notice small movement lines around the animals at first, leading to the explosion of cartoon fight devices in frame four.

◀ RACHAEL BALL
Absence of dialogue makes this sequence enigmatic and ambiguous, as in a dream where logic and realism cannot be counted on. The color gives the images a lush personality, using a family of colors to mesh the shapes and textures. The smooth, translucent color of felt-tip pens is combined with rough-textured colored pencil work and fine ink outlines and hatching.

► NICK ABADZIS
Modern cartoons have increasingly used simplified drawing and storytelling formats to make serious comment. But cartoonists can make a doubly subversive message by also mocking their own commentary, so the viewer picks up layers of irony. Here, ridiculous cartoon devices are used to characterize aspects of the sheep's appearance and behavior.

▲ SHAUN HAYES-HOLGATE
Illustration of a narrative poem creates a page crammed with activity, in both text and images. To clarify the storyline, most of the poem has been typeset, except for some dialogue, which is integrated with the pictures as direct speech balloons. But the artist also includes jokes and comments that satirize the poem, among drawings densely filled with varied stylistic devices, including a secondary layer of illustration in the caption boxes.

▲ BRAD TEARE
In an interesting variation on black-and-white technique, the artist has used scratchboard for the image, which means bringing the whites out of a black ink layer rather than drawing positive blacks. The slanted, stacked arrangement of the page resembles the pyramid of rocks in the story. A simplified color palette adds depth and richness, allowing the speech balloons to float. The distinctive lettering style is part of the characterization of the narrator figure.

▲ GRAHAM HIGGINS
Varying the panels so inventively in both scale and content creates a strip packed with incident. The drawing is imaginative, but has a cohesive style that keeps it all together. The outer mini-panels, like little movie-film frames, and the artist's introduction of his own drawing hand point out the essential non-realism of comic action.

SHOPPING for CATS

◀◀ ANNIE LAWSON
Not only is the main character in this strip pared down to the bare essentials, the precise context of the situation is withheld until the last possible moment. But it states a universally recognizable dilemma for which the reader can propose a personal background narrative.

◀ ANNIE LAWSON
The interesting "disconnected" style of drawing gives only the briefest explanation of scale and space, so the setting is read as a flat visual pattern which gradually breaks into separate components. The words carry greater weight than in some cartoon forms as the drawing does not make the joke explicit.

▶ SUZY VARTY
The apparent subject of this cartoon provides an oblique way of commenting on the actual subject, both having a personal and more broadly cultural context. The stylishly drawn cartoon has an excellent balance of black and white, but it is the simple, vivid color blocks which give it great impact.

▼ MAGGIE LING
This strip is driven by the script, and in a way would work just as well if it were a radio monologue, but the character is drawn in an accomplished, characterful manner. The artist uses the simplified features and cropped figure very expressively.

Young Telegraph
Number 2

Professor Questertester SOLVES THE MYSTERIES OF THE UNIVERSE © WAGNER GRANT Hughes

◀ RIAN HUGHES

For a strip that runs in the young reader's section of a national newspaper, the plain, direct styling of large shapes and a simple tonal range creates an allover design effect that is easily accessible. The narrative is a spoof on the idea of educational cartoons, using joke information.

▶ HUNT EMERSON

The running theme of swarms makes the frames fill up very quickly, so that the drawing soon creates a massed pattern effect. The individual characters get progressively harder to see, though their simple shapes work in line or silhouette. Emphasis is achieved through varying line weights and reducing specific detail within the swarm where it would become too confusing.

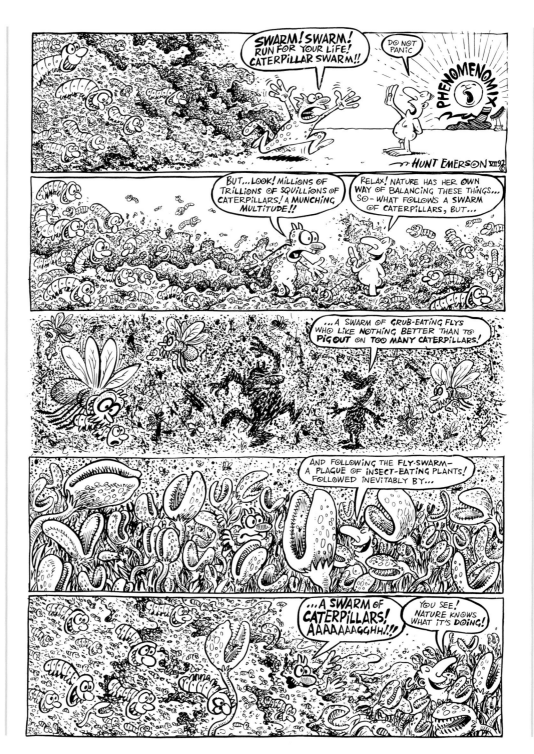

BRIAN BOLLAND
▲ A strip commenting
satirically on various aspects of
English weather, countryside,
and vacation pursuits uses a
finely drawn, consistent style of
line work to describe character,
mood, and atmospherics.

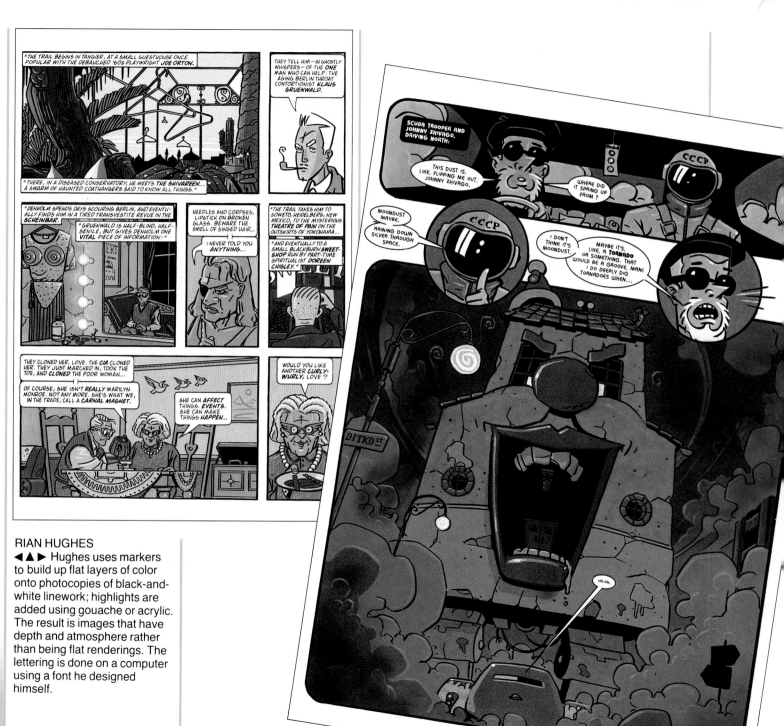

RIAN HUGHES

◄▲► Hughes uses markers to build up flat layers of color onto photocopies of black-and-white linework; highlights are added using gouache or acrylic. The result is images that have depth and atmosphere rather than being flat renderings. The lettering is done on a computer using a font he designed himself.

A cartoon that illustrates something is not a difficult concept to grasp. It is less clear where a cartoon stops being definable as such and simply becomes a commissioned illustration in an artist's particular style. Sometimes a jokey, simplified image is needed, which is the natural area of cartooning. At other times, the illustration may appear clearer or better suited to the style and content of the text it accompanies if it uses some of the techniques and devices that are associated with cartoons.

To some extent, in this area, it is up to the artist to decide whether or not the picture "qualifies" as a cartoon. But if a cartoon-like style is wanted, it makes better sense to use a professional who is accustomed to interpreting images this way, than to ask a general illustrator to try to imitate it. Cartoon illustrations are commissioned for magazines and books, as cover pictures and to be integrated with text, and also for advertising purposes, such as in brochures, mailshots, and handouts.

▲ LARRY
The weightlifter dominates the image by his size, and the eye level of all other characters aligns with the autograph book he is holding. There are two essential props, the barbell tucked under his chin and the autograph book, which is labeled, so the cartoon needs no caption. Notice how the heaviness of the weights is emphasized by downward, hatched shading, while everything else has a horizontal or slanted emphasis.

▶ DUSAN POLAKOVIC
The linear work in this picture describing the straining book spines and pressurizing screw threads is all to the benefit of its "squeeze" effect. The lines form subtly varied tonal shading and pull the eye to the center of the image, where the dense liquid forms a solid black shape. This is all focused very directly by centering the composition and isolating it within its frame.

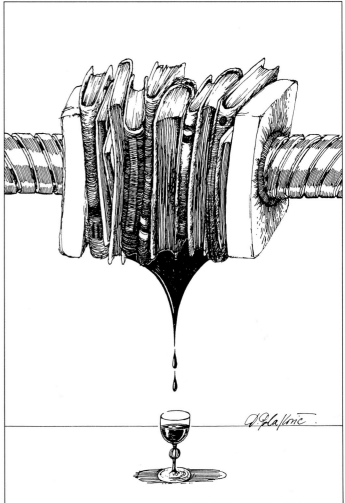

◀ TED DEWAN
Lithographic crayon shaded over textured paper creates deep, soft tones giving depth to the pen drawing. Sharp white highlighting, some applied in process white, adds to mood and dimension. The subject of the cartoon is loss of arts funding, hence the destructive sawing of the cello which bears monetary symbols.

▼ TORMA LACO
Excellent use of hatching creates space and depth. The diminishing scale of the brick walls is controlled by careful line work, but the drawing has energy and textural interest. The fruit on the distant tree, the reward for getting through the maze, is unnaturally large in scale, so it is identifiable.

◄ TED DEWAN
Giving human attributes to inanimate objects is not an easy task. The artist has solved it here in two ways, by animating the actual forms of the telephones and by adding humanoid limbs. The dancing rhythm of the line drawing and intense crayon shading with high contrasts of tone make the image leap into three dimensions.

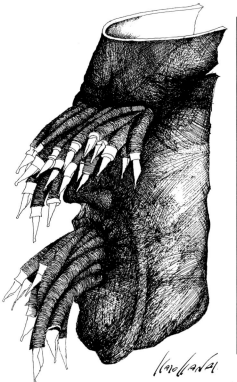

◄ KAZO KANALA
This surreal portrait depends on a bizarre juxtaposition of elements. The pens exude from eyes and mouth, both organs of communication, but the shapes are limp and the drawing has a dark, despairing mood. Fine, tightly knitted crosshatching creates dramatic modeling.

► DANIEL
The chef's culinary achievement is subtly understated, almost lost amid the clutter of the kitchen, described with amusing detail. The composition is loosely structured around an inverted triangle that leads the eye down to the hard-cooked egg proudly displayed by the cook. More literally, the focus of attention is signaled by his hand gesture.

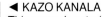

▲ STEFANO TOGNETTI
Taking the popular cartoon figure Tintin and drawing him in a style unlike his own is an example of direct homage often seen in illustrational cartoons. The color scheme is in fact quite close to that of the original books; color consistency is among the elements that aid recognition.

▲ BRYAN TALBOT
A central theme of this image is light, portrayed in different ways both figuratively and narratively. The intensity of light within the room comes from the artist's boldness in using dramatic tonal contrasts, and areas which lack detail within a heavily detailed rendering.

These shapes are freely formed by tonal gradation or anchored by subtle line work. Behind the journalist lighting a cigarette hangs Holman Hunt's famous picture *The Light of the World,* a religious icon which counterpoints the man's squalid surroundings and cynical expression.

▲ RIAN HUGHES
Bold paper cutout shapes and strong grainy drawing make a powerful, "quick" image that is highly self-descriptive and relates immediately to the editorial context of a feature on insurance coverage for sports injuries.

▶ JULIE HOLLINGS
This is a directly illustrative image for a feature on body oils that would work extremely well in black and white, but the loosely brushed, bright colors are an eye-catching bonus.

Are your patients getting disorderly?

B
CNF
APHO
YTDM7O

If so, Imtec has the answer . . .

▲ SAX
In this advertising illustration, caption copy puts across the exact context, and the artist is free to develop the complex detail of a crowded situation, bringing in witty, almost overlooked details like the figure crammed into the filing drawer.

▲ JIM WHITING
Designed as a vignette for a book cover, this illustration is consistently related to the outer oval, not only in the directional shapes of the figure and his surroundings, but in the way the hatching fades into an open white, spotlit center.

UG...GRUNT FNIK AR SNURT!✱

◄ JULIE HOLLINGS
A commission for book illustration gives a cartoonist room to associate freely, since the drawings can make comments of their own which may or may not relate directly to the surrounding text. This feminist cartoon synthesizes old and new cultural stereotypes.

✱ TRANSLATES AS: 'THESE TWO WILL BE NICE ROASTED WITH A FEW HERBS!'

NOTE: Page numbers in *italics* denote illustrations in Themes section

M

N

O

P

R

S

CREDITS

We would like to thank the many contributors who have kindly allowed us to reproduce their work in this book; thanks are also due to Nick Abadzis, Rachel Ball, Tony Banks, Bojan M! Djukic, Simon Ellinas of Squigglers, Carl Flint, David Lewis, Peter Maddocks, Woodrow Phoenix, Paul 'Mooncat' Schroeder, Ross Thomson, Ron Tiner, and Steve Whitaker for illustration work in the Techniques section. We are also indebted to Carol Bennett of Knockabout, London, and Paul Gravett at the Cartoon Art Trust, London, for their help during our research; and to Langford & Hill, who loaned tools and equipment for photography.

The following artists' work appears by kind permission of Anthony Brandt Artists' Agent, Chesham House, 150 Regent Street, London W1R 5FA: Albert, Banx, Bill Caldwell, Camley, Karl Dixon, Pat Drennan, Emms, Roland Fiddy, Haldane, Julie Hollings, Larry, McLachlan, Don Roberts, Sax, Clive Wafker, Mike Williams.

Key: a = above b = below
c = center l = left r = right

Pages 1, 2, 3, 8, 9 Peter Maddocks; page 22/3 Peter Maddocks; page 33br Moira Clinch; page 44bl Rebecca Horsewood; page 52cr Stefano Tognetti; pages 73br, 81b Peter Maddocks; page 89b Marty Murphy; page 96 Ron Tiner; page 99b Bill Caldwell; page 100b Clive Collins; pages 103b, 104bc Peter Maddocks; page 104br portfolio work by Hunt Emerson and Brian Bolland; page 104ar letterheads courtesy of Steve Whitaker, and Squigglers; pages 106/107 illustration by Ross Thomson, taken from *Dog Facts* by Joan Palmer, published 1991 by Stanley Paul (UK) and Barnes & Noble (US); page 112b Dan Spiegle; page 113l Nick Abadzis; page 113r Peter Maddocks; page 114ar Brian Bolland © DC Comics Inc; bl from *Video Max* © Origa/Ambrosini/Fumetti d'Italia; br Nick Abadzis; page 115tr Dan Spiegle; bc David Lloyd, from *The Pencil* by Raymond Chandler, art © 1994 Byron Preiss Visual Publications;

page 117 Nick Abadzis; page 118ar Daniel; cr Marty Murphy; page 119br Dan Spiegle; page 120/1 from *How to Draw and Sell Comic Strips* by Alan McKenzie, published in 1987 by Macdonald Orbis (UK) and Northlight (US); pages 124/5 Peter Maddocks; 135r from *Animal Man* © DC Comics Inc; page 149l © DC Comics Inc; page 151a Peter Clarke appears by courtesy of *The Guardian*; pages 152, 153a from *Batman* © DC Comics Inc; page 153bl from *Crisis* © Fleetway Editions Ltd; page 155r characters © 1993 Oakley & D'Israeli, reproduced by kind permission of Deadline Publications Ltd; page 162 © Wagner Grant (words); page 165 © Fleetway Editions Ltd and used with permission; pages 172–6 Peter Maddocks.